"Travis Rogers has done the pro-life movement a real service in writing *Unaborted Truth*. Filled with practical argumentation based on real conversation with abortion proponents, he provides detailed answers to common objections that will help anyone involved in defending the pro-life position in public, whether on the political left or from so called "abortion abolitionists." *Unaborted Truth* is a must read!"
Scott J. Mahurin, Director, Florida Preborn Rescue

"In order for pro-lifers to succeed in our goal of legally protecting preborn children, it is imperative that we make compelling arguments. As such, *Unaborted Truth* by Travis Rogers is a great resource for anyone interested in pro-life apologetics. It contains persuasive theological and philosophical arguments for the sanctity of all human life. It also contains a section of conversations where Rogers skillfully uses pro-life apologetics to dialogue with individuals who support legal abortion. Overall, *Unaborted Truth* is a must read for pro-lifers."
Michael New, Research Associate, The Catholic University of America and Director, Washington, DC 40 Days for Life Campaign

"In *Unaborted Truth*, Travis Rogers has provided a valuable resource to Christians who struggle with sharing their pro-life views or answering pro-choice objections. The material in this book supplies a basic apologetic for participating in this impassioned debate effectively. If you are looking for help to fortify your engagement, read this book."
Steve Clevenger, Pastor, Covenant Reformed Baptist Church, Warrenton, VA

"Travis Rogers takes an in-depth and systematic approach to the critical dispute of abortion. There are golden nuggets of truth for the seasoned veteran and new pursuers of truth. Don't miss out, *Unaborted Truth* is very readable! I devoured the book in just two evenings."
Troy Newman, President, Operation Rescue

Travis W. Rogers

Unaborted Truth

Logical Arguments for Life

Travis W. Rogers

ISBN-13: 979-8-5322-3046-0

DEDICATION

To my dear brother in Christ, Stephen Balloon. Your steadfast devotion to Christ, and your unwavering devotion to the preborn, is an encouragement beyond words. For years, you've been committed to proclaiming the gospel outside of our local abortion mill, and it has been an honor to go with you when possible. Stay firm in the faith and in your convictions, brother!

CONTENTS

Acknowledgments   i

Introduction   ii

1   What is Man?   1

2   Common Pro-Choice Objections   7

2.1   Keep Religion Out of It   8

2.2   Clump of Cells   10

2.3   Not a Person   17

2.4   It's Legal   21

2.5   Unwanted   23

2.6   Rape, Incest, & Genetics   24

2.7   I Can't Afford a Baby!   28

2.8   Better Than Coat Hangers   32

2.9   My Body, My Choice!   36

3   Pro-Life, Abolition, & Theonomy   47

APPENDICES

A   Abortion: An Illogical and Unethical Conclusion   67

B   Real Talk   79

C   Pregnancy Resources   159

ACKNOWLEDGMENTS

As the years have gone by, one thing has remained constant. I've always had an amazing group of people surrounding me, offering encouragement in a moment of need and accountability in a moment of growth. For this, I am forever thankful. Above all else, I am thankful for my beautiful bride and three amazing children who continually provide me with laughs, love, and lessons on life. By God's grace, He has gifted me with a household that trusts my leadership as I seek Christ's headship through prayer and the study of the Word.

INTRODUCTION

In an era where speaking out against the masses is enough to have one ostracized, why on earth would I be crazy enough to want to discuss the topic of abortion? After all, it would be much easier to just go with the flow and choose not to offend. It seems those opposed to abortion face constant ridicule and are viewed as supporting a violation of civil rights, inhibiting women's healthcare, and promoting the patriarchy. So, I ask again, why on earth would I be crazy enough to write about it? The answer is simple: human lives are on the line. It is nothing short of this. For all the points being made, no point is greater than the millions of lives lost. In this work, I seek to address some of the common points used by the pro-choice community. If you do not know the arguments employed, you will be ill-equipped to combat them. As such, you will find real conversations in the appendix. While the main portion of the book is a systematic breakdown of arguments and varying positions within both the pro-choice and pro-life camps, I felt it would be beneficial to see how these points are brought to life in the practical sense. By finding life in the argument, perhaps we can eventually find a push for life within humanity at large.

"For You formed my inward parts; You wove me in my mother's womb."
Psalm 139:13

Travis W. Rogers

1 WHAT IS MAN?

What is man? Of all the questions that could be asked to start off the topic, I believe this question to be of the utmost importance if we have any desire to untangle the web of points and counterpoints that we all encounter when debating abortion. We could try to bring it back further and begin with evidence of life, but I am convinced that would be to put the cart before the horse. We are not merely arguing for life. We are arguing for human life. All life is important, but not all life is equally valuable. For instance, I greatly enjoy eating bacon with my eggs. The pig, while very much having had a valid life, held a different value than that of a human enjoying a nice breakfast. Thus, I return to my original question: What is man?

Genesis 1:27

> God created man in His own image, in the image of God He created him; male and female He created them.

According to Scripture, mankind was made on the sixth day of creation. While God created all that is *ex nihilo* (Latin for "out of nothing"), He made the first man, Adam, from the dust of the earth. Upon being created, God breathed life into Adam. First Corinthians 15:45 provides clarification of Genesis 2:7 where it states that Adam "became of living soul." The purpose of this book is not to delve into the intricacies of the soul, nor to be an exposition of the *imago Dei*. I begin with this to set the framework for how we Christians should approach the topic. Certainly, unbelievers can argue for life, and many do. More about that can be found in later chapters. However, as believers, we are to reason with the mind of Christ (1 Corinthians 2:16). Therefore, having at least a cursory understanding of what took place at creation, and why mankind is set apart from all else, is critical if we hope to be consistent and systematic.

The London Baptist Confession of Faith, published in 1689, in the beginning of chapter 4, states:

> After God had made all other creatures, he created man, male and female, with reasonable and immortal souls, rendering them fit unto that life to God for which they were created; being made in the image of God, in knowledge, righteousness and true holiness; having the law of God written in their hearts.[i]

Accordingly, it is the very image of God that enables us to live the life God intended. By our unique ability to reason, and our obligation to worship our Creator, we are distinct from the rest of creation. The image of God is not just something we possess. It is the essence of our being and constitutes our identity. Although we may be in a fallen state, we are still made in the very image and likeness of God. We bear His image and are morally obligated to be like Him.[ii] Simply put, we are to be holy because He is holy (1 Peter 1:16).

Being image bearers of God is not to be taken lightly. It is something we are all involved in at a fundamental level of our very being. But what of the unbeliever who rejects God? Is there any ground to assert that he still has such a moral obligation? The simple answer to that is a resounding yes! He may reject God, as many do, but that does not free a person from that obligation. Scripture is clear that all have sinned (Romans 3:23) and that the wages of sin is death

(Romans 6:23). A lack of faith in God does not nullify the image unbelievers bear. Believers and unbelievers alike are charged with being holy. The difference is that, without Christ, unbelievers inevitably fail in their quest for self-awareness and self-help (Romans 1:16-32).

The difficult part is not in justifying why the unbeliever still owes God the same honor and worship as the believer. The difficult part is in convincing such a person of this fact. The secular person has quite different values than the Christian. This stems from a difference in worldview. We see value in life because God made it. We find special value in human life because God breathed into us and created us to be moral agents. The unbeliever has suppressed this truth (Romans 1:18) and attempted to replace God's order with his own. It is in this attempt that we see mankind having value ascribed by fellow man, rather than being inherent. Under this construct, people are deemed only as valuable as culture determines them to be. There is no absolute standard, moral code, or value system.

If atheism were true, a case could clearly be made for such a system. In such a state of existence, there is no purpose and no value. We would all be nothing more than cosmic dust, randomly formed into what we are. Emotional connections would be nothing more than electronic pulses firing between synapses of a randomly generated brain. As famed atheist Richard Dawkins has admitted,

> "In a universe of electrons and selfish genes, blind physical forces and genetic replication, some people are going to get hurt, other people are going to get lucky, and you won't find any rhyme or reason in it, nor any justice. The universe that we observe has precisely the properties we should expect if there is, at bottom, no design, no purpose, no evil, no good, nothing but pitiless indifference."[iii]

He goes on to succinctly state, "DNA neither knows nor cares. DNA just is. And we dance to its music."[iv] Apart from God, life is meaningless. There is no purpose, no value, no joy, no logic, no

3

relations, and no reason. Anything ascribed to any facet of life is nothing more than the fanciful and inconsistent whims of a sentient and collective form of space dust. The only difference between man and a candy wrapper is the candy wrapper at least has purpose because it was created by someone with intent. In such a system, the only consistent form of living would be pure and unadulterated nihilism. But this is not the case. In fact, I know many atheists who are more caring than some self-professing Christians. This is because, while claiming there is no God, they borrow from the Christian worldview that says each person has inherent value from being created in the *imago Dei*. They seek to retain the dignity that only exists among those who bear God's image, while denying Him. This dignity only exists because God has granted it to us through His image. He takes it so seriously, He has decreed that the man who sheds the blood of one made in His image shall be put to death (Genesis 9:6).

We can justify relationships on a human level because of the very God who created us to worship Him on a relational level. Worship is not meant to be stoic but should be filled with joy and exuberance as we exalt our Creator, who made us in His image. Because we are made to be relational beings as well as moral agents, this must determine how we approach the topic of abortion. After all, how can one created in the image of God idly stand by and watch as millions of other image bearers are led to the slaughter and cast aside as nothing more than a hollow idea that will never come to fruition? Abortion does far more than just kill unborn humans. It seeks to undo the *imago Dei*, while telling the world there is no God and no righteous standard. Such an idea should fill us with righteous anger and remorse for the sinful world in which we live. In one fell swoop, secular culture has become an affront to both God and His image. Perhaps more than ever, we are now at a time where we need to rethink who we are…who God created us to be. In solidarity, we need to stand for biblical truth in the face of adversity while becoming a voice for the voiceless.

The pro-choice movement has made significant inroads because of their solidarity and patience. While not all people in this movement share the same values, or even the same reasons for supporting the movement, they all stand united for their cause. Whether it be bodily autonomy, or a sick sense of getting away with legal murder, pro-choicers stand together for abortion-on-demand. However, the pro-life community has proven time and again that such solidarity seems to be just out of reach (see more in Chapter 3). Imagine what could be accomplished if we set aside our differences and came together in the fight to end abortion.

Unfortunately, I have stood side-by-side with an atheist as we attempted to convince a third party of the atrocities of abortion, only to be rebuked by a fellow Christian because my methodology differed. This lack of unity has become our undoing, and resulted in the death of over 50 million image bearers in the U.S. since 1973,[v] and up to an estimated 2 billion worldwide.[vi] There is enough opposition out there already. We shouldn't be creating new enemies just for the sake of our pride. We shouldn't be looking to create enemies at all.

When we evangelize, we are met with resistance. As the gospel goes forth, resistance always follows. While we have a biblical warrant to rebuke false teachers, most unbelievers are simply lost in their suppression of the truth. While fallen human nature precludes any possibility of a neutral position before God, ignorance is still very real. Similarly, many who support abortion-on-demand do so because they are not convinced that the preborn are children in need of saving. Even when addressing groups such as NARAL, some members likely believe they are actually standing up against oppression. By all means, condemn the group and stand firm for truth, but always remember to season our words with salt so that we might know how to properly respond in grace (Colossians 4:6). This is why I have no qualms about calling abortion murder and calling people out of their sin, yet I will not go around screaming, "Murderer," at women who enter an abortion facility. It is counterproductive and contrary to the prescribed manner of speech found in Scripture. Ultimately, our goal must not be to only save physical lives but spiritual lives as well. The former can occur through protest and changes in law, but the latter will only occur through the spread of the gospel as we shine the light of Christ in the dark alleys of deceit and despair.

Much of the remainder of this book will be dedicated to addressing the logical inconsistencies of the arguments used in the pro-choice camp. After all, the very subtitle of this book is "Logical Arguments for Life." This is why I felt the need to begin by providing a biblical understanding of who we are as created beings. If you are a believer, I urge you to use this understanding as the foundation for why you fight against abortion. If you are an unbeliever, I pray for the eternal state of your soul, and hope the above comment gives you something to chew on. I also thank you for your efforts in standing up for the rights of the preborn and hope to keep you as an ally in the fight against this latest form of genocide.

---

[i] The 1689 Baptist Confession of Faith, Chapter 4 - Of Creation, Paragraph 2

[ii] Samuel E. Waldron, *A Modern Exposition of the 1689 Baptist Confession of Faith, Third Edition* [Durham: Evangelical Press, 1999] 84-85

[iii] Richard Dawkins, *River out of Eden: A Darwinian View of Life* [New York: Basic Books, 1995] 132-133

[iv] ibid, 133

[v] Centers for Disease Control and Prevention, *Data and Statistics.* https://www.cdc.gov/reproductivehealth/data_stats/index.htm

[vi] Colin Mason and Stephen Mosher, "Earth Day: Abortion has killed 1-2 billion worldwide in 50 years," *Life Site News*, 21 April 2011, https://www.lifenews.com/2011/04/21/earth-day-abortion-has-killed-1-2-billion-worldwide-in-50-years/

2 COMMON PRO-CHOICE OBJECTIONS

In my years of discussing this topic with others, I have yet to find a consistent argument for abortion-on-demand. By no means do I consider myself the standard against which to measure truth or consistency, but I do admit my own experiences have caused me to yearn for some form of intelligible response. With how widespread abortion has become since its legalization on January 22, 1973, combined with the ferocity in which pro-choicers argued in favor of it, one would think a sound argument would have developed by now. However, in all I have seen and heard, my experience says that is not the case.

The only consistency within the movement appears to be consistently shifting the goalposts while being consistently inconsistent. Instead of addressing the subject at hand – the inherent value and dignity of human life – the pool has become flooded with red herrings and the field littered with strawmen. That said, some are admittedly more cleverly disguised than others. Just as is the case with any error, some will captivate while others will repugnate. Because of this, we must look at each argument carefully and find that loose thread that will unravel it. You may not see it, but it is there. After all, when something is in opposition to God, how can it be logically or morally consistent?

Instead of cluttering this book with unnecessary chapter divisions, each argument will instead be broken out by headings within this main chapter. For your convenience and easy reference, the Table of Contents will refer to each argument individually and will give the corresponding page number. With that said, let us dive into some of the most common pro-choice objections and arguments I have encountered over the years.

2.1 KEEP RELIGION OUT OF IT

This may be the most common objection I have ever heard. Of course, it is entirely understandable. After all, if I were to tell you there was a group of people protesting outside the local abortion mill, and I were to ask you to guess their organization, you would probably assume it was a group of Christians from a local church, or maybe a religious pro-life organization banding together. You would probably be correct.

However, just because a group of protesters is primarily Christian, does this give credence to the argument that our position is solely religious? Yes and no. If we hope to be consistent (remember that pesky term?), everything we say and do should be for God's glory. In that sense, everything in our lives should come from our devotion to Christ and service to Him. But that doesn't automatically disqualify us from the fight. Remember, it is people's suppression of God's truth that makes them inconsistent. In the strictest sense, both sides are arguing from their religious perspectives: one for God and the other against Him. So long as either party holds to any values whatsoever, there is still room for both to come to the table with their arguments.

Perhaps today more than ever before, politics has consumed us as a people. Whereas party labels used to be how we registered to vote, they have since become much more. During my high school days, I remember overhearing a fellow student asking our teacher what political party he was affiliated with. The student was curious and there was no way to know other than to ask. While there are still some who hold to traditional party affiliations and traditions, most are now open with their politics.

Let us follow the same format given above. If I were to present to you a person who was an advocate for the LGBTQ, sought to implement Democratic Socialism (an oxymoron, if you ask me), sided with abortion-on-demand, and wanted universal healthcare, what party do you think he would associate with? In fact, I would be willing to bet your answer would remain the same even if it were only one of those instances. Now, let's say there is a person who is for traditional marriage, capitalism, or the eradication of abortion, what party are you guessing? While it is not a guarantee, and surface-level assumptions are always a bad idea, there is a strong probability that you would be right.

Seemingly gone are the days of keeping our voter registration card hidden away in our wallet. These days, it is practically tattooed on the arms of everyone with an internet connection. Fueled by the political agendas of the mainstream media, you don't have to look far to find a polarizing topic, along with advocates for each side. We have all become political pundits with a doctorate in keyboard warfare.

So, what does that mean for the supposition that being pro-life is purely a religious matter? It means there is no merit to the claim. While a love for or disdain of God will always be the underlying motivating factor, the argument has become equally as political on both sides. Furthermore, it is rooted in empirical evidence and can be argued from a purely intellectual position should one desire to do so. Reverend Frank Pavone made this point very clear in his logical breakdown of fundamental human rights:

> "A fundamental right is a human right without which we cannot express out humanity. At the top of the list are life itself and liberty. We cannot live as fully functioning persons if we are enslaved. A person, by definition, by his or her very nature, is free...And yet to be free, a person must first be alive. To deprive a person of life is to deprive a person of liberty. It

stands to reason, literally, that the very right to life has to be respected and protected. Life is an even more fundamental right than freedom...To hold the state accountable for protecting those fundamental rights has nothing to do with imposing religious beliefs and everything to do with reason."[i]

As Janet Morana has said, "That a unique human life begins at conception is a scientific fact, not a religious argument."[ii]

2.2 CLUMP OF CELLS

Why should we care what someone chooses to do with a clump of cells? Where is the outrage over nail clippings and haircuts? Why are we not protesting the surgical removal of dangerous cells within a cancer patient? If the preborn are truly just a clump of cells, and there is already a medical precedent for removing unwanted cells, on what ground do we dare say abortion is a moral and societal evil?

Truth be told, this argument is too volatile for most pro-choicers to use anymore. The entire argument hinges upon when life begins. While it is still commonly used on social media, it is no longer in the arsenal of most skeptics, and for good reason. Most no longer employ this argument because of the scientific fact that all living tissue is made of cells. Physically, I am nothing more than the culmination of nearly four decades of cell development. The plant on my fireplace mantle is also comprised of living cells. The key component to this is that, for cells to exist, there must be biological life. Thus, the argument must narrow its scope to the kind of life in question.

Going back to the example of cancer, those deadly cells, while coming from a human, are not, and never will become, human. It doesn't matter how long you wait. Cancer cells will always be cancer cells. Similarly, a baby's first hair clippings will never begin to cry from within the pages of the baby book in which it is taped. Yet, if the pregnant human body is left to function in its natural capacity, from conception to delivery, the cells will continue to collect, reproduce, and grow into a unique human being with a unique genetic code. Additionally, this genetic code is determined at the time of conception when the 23 chromosomes carried by the sperm combine with the 23 chromosomes carried by the egg.[iii] In other words, science dictates that human life begins at conception.

As expected, this has only caused the goalposts to shift even further. Instead of arguing against life, the popular argument is now against personhood. While we will return to this later, I would like to stay with the current theme a bit longer. Since science dictates when life begins, any opposition becomes an argument against science, not against pro-life advocacy. There are still those who will admit that the zygote, blastocyst, embryo, and fetus are human life while denying the inherent value and dignity of that life. They attempt to adhere to the "clump of cells" argument by opting to qualify what it means to be human. This has only led them into a slew of other problems that are rooted in their refuge of delusional semantics[iv] and redefining of terms. I agree with Dr. Tommy Mitchell in his bold proclamation, "We dare not play word games with human life to justify personal agendas."[v]

Each of the above terms (i.e. zygote, blastocyst, embryo, and fetus) are words used to describe the various stages of human life. None of them have anything to do with determining the beginning of life. They merely describe the development of the preborn human in the womb.[vi] It is akin to our accepted concept of later human development in how we speak of newborns, infants, toddlers, teenagers, middle-aged, and elderly persons. It is not a new concept. If it can be, and is, applied to the born, there is zero reason for such resistance in applying it to the preborn, other than an innate hardness of the heart and the inability to accept the truth.

Truly, if you ask a pro-choicer when life begins, you will hear anything from conception to the first breath. Despite their solidarity for the end objective, there seems to be no consensus when it comes to the finer points. Moving forward, I would like to address some of the stages of human development and why you might hear such a stage being arbitrarily chosen as the delineation of when life begins. Please keep in mind that the only differences between the preborn and the born are matters of physical maturity and where one resides.[vii]

POST-EARLY STAGES

Those who hold to the position that human life does not begin until later in pregnancy tend to use miscarriage as their guiding standard. The claim is that, if approximately 10-20 percent of pregnancies end in miscarriage, with most being in the first trimester, the zygote, blastocyst, or embryo truly cannot yet be human. However, tragedy does not nullify existence. All it means is the preborn child, while fighting for survival at a cellular level, did not make it out alive. God created us as complex organisms. Fetal development is no exception. The same argument is employed, using implantation as a guide. For instance, if uterine implantation never occurs, it is argued that the fertilized egg no longer has the potential for becoming life. Yet, implantation does not cause life. It only helps ensure its survival.[viii]

Others have attempted to use cases of twins in an attempt to deny humanity in the early stages. After all, if humanity (not to be confused with humanness) begins at fertilization, it would dictate that the zygote or embryo is a unique individual. Yet, twins would seemingly defy such a claim. Up until roughly the 14th day, the cells can still split, and twins can now exist. This, they claim, means there would now be two distinct personalities and people even though there was only one before. The argument is that, while being proof of life, it is not proof of humanity, which they believe comes after the twinning process has completed. However, there are cases where the twinning process never completes, and the cells remain in a partial split state. This results in what is known as conjoined twins. Conjoined twins are two distinct personalities even though they never completed the cellular twinning process and will even share body parts or organs. Thus, while it is not definitive proof that humanity begins at conception, it is proof that a zygote need not complete the twinning process for humanity to exist.[ix]

POINT OF VIABILITY

To add yet another view into the mix, there is the position that the fetus is not actually a life until the point of viability. "Point of viability" is the term used to define when a fetus is capable of survival in the event of a premature birth. According to this view, the fetus is incapable of surviving on its own outside of the womb. Thus, there is no moral obligation to protect it inside the womb since it is not yet a viable life. As with the other points, this argument holds no water.

First, this standard is not applied to anything else in life. If I get dropped in the middle of the jungle, the chances of my survival are going to be fairly slim as opposed to my current living situation. If I am alone in the jungle, does this make me less human than if I were at home? To this, some will reply by saying I at least have a chance of survival. The fetus, they say, has zero chance of survival without some form of human interaction and intervention, making it fully dependent upon another for survival. While this is true, it changes nothing. A newborn also has zero chance of survival if left alone following birth.[x] With all three of my children, aside from me cutting the umbilical cord, one of the first things done was the nurse clearing the airway of amniotic fluid. Then, after their first bath, they put salve over their eyes, and wrapped them in a blanket. Over the course of many sleepless nights, our babies all cried when hungry, needed to be fed, and desired to be comforted. As any parent can attest, all newborns are dependent upon someone else for survival. If left alone, their chance of survival is absolutely zero. Yet, by the standard of argumentation being employed within the pro-choice camp, a newborn would now have to be considered non-viable. Yes, he or she may live slightly longer than a preborn child who is less physically mature, but the fact remains that the newborn is not capable of sustaining life and will certainly die if left alone. Heaven forbid that a newborn has a medical condition at birth.

That makes the child even less viable. If non-viable, the door now opens to legal infanticide. Thankfully, inconsistency is being chosen in this case. As it stands, chance of survival does not dictate or define humanity. It only contributes to one's quality and longevity of life.

Secondly, with advances in medical technology, the point of viability has shifted. The point of viability is now considered to be 24 weeks gestation.[xi] In 1973, the consensus was that it could be as late as 28 weeks before the fetus achieved viability. However, in 2014, a baby was successfully delivered at only 21 weeks and weighed less than a pound.[xii] Clearly, a linear line in the sand is nothing more than an arbitrary delineation based on probability in an ever-changing medical scene. This is not a time of war where a swarm of combat patients are in triage, while only those with the best chances of survival are able to be treated. We are talking about whether or not a mother should have the right to kill her child based on mere statistical probability. Once again, chance of survival does not define humanity. As said by Dr. Tommy Mitchell:

> "Proponents of the ecological view hold that the fetus is human when it reaches a level of maturation when it can exist outside of the mother's womb...The problem is that, over the last century, we have been becoming human earlier and earlier. Here the issue is not the actual stage of development of the fetus. The limiting factor is the current state of medical technology."[xiii]

GEOGRAPHICAL LOCATION

Furthermore, depending on where you live, your care may be better or worse than that of another. If a 28-week pregnant woman lives in New York City, she will likely have access to cutting edge medical technology and a host of skilled doctors. At this point, nearly all would agree that her child is viable. However, what if she were to fly to a remote village in Africa for a trip? While there is a possibility of survival, the chances plummet. Certainly, the term "point of viability" would no longer apply. Now, let us assume she flies back home safely and is now at 29 weeks gestation. Once again, her fetus is considered viable. Does this mean her unborn child went from being human, to non-human, and back to human again, all in the span of one week? What a ludicrous thought! Not only is it ludicrous, but it is also dehumanizing. Such a hateful attitude should not be tolerated.

FIRST BREATH

Going all the way to the right of the prenatal timeline, we encounter the birth of the child. While most will agree that life begins at some point in the womb, even if that point is not unilaterally agreed upon, there are many who hold to the belief that life begins at the first breath and ends with the last breath. This takes the "clump of cells" position to the extreme as level of development plays no part in determining life. The zygote at one day into the gestational process is just as inhuman has the 38 week gestational fetus who is just waiting for cervical dilation and uterine contractions. Such views have only paved the way for talks of partial-birth abortion where a matter of six inches (average length of the birth canal) determines life. Even worse, if held to a consistent standard, it would actually open up talks of killing the birthed baby so long as the first breath was not yet taken.

Not only is this view one of the most dangerous, it is also highly inconsistent. The entire purpose of cardiopulmonary resuscitation (CPR) is to attempt to help a person resume breathing. However, if one has ceased breathing, this standard would have to consider the victim to be dead, and CPR would no longer be necessary. If we have an entire medical procedure dedicated to saving lives and providing breathing assistance, why is that same kind of dedication not applied to the fetus? During the height of the COVID-19 pandemic, the headlines were littered with hospitals requesting additional ventilators due to patients being unable to breathe on their own. These respirators would, in effect, breathe on behalf of patients by pumping air in and out of their lungs. At this point, the person is no longer breathing of their own accord. While COVID-19 has claimed many lives, simply being hooked up to a ventilator is not considered a COVID-related death. At this point, the patient is incapable of breathing but is still very much alive. If breathing machines and CPR are acceptable measures to help someone continue breathing, we can certainly have the same expectation that it be applied to assist the fetus in breathing. No medical standard exists that would declare a victim to be dead solely because he has stopped breathing. The ability to breathe does not dictate life.

Taking the previous statement to a practical level, imagine a free diver who can hold his breath for upwards of eight minutes. What happens if he goes too deep and does not allow time to resurface? Is he considered dead at the point of drowning or did he die eight minutes earlier when he took his last breath? Again, it just does not make any sense. Regarding the COVID-19 example, if one believes the preborn are not alive due to lacking the ability to breathe, such a person must also advocate the slaughter of hospital patients hooked up to ventilators.

Furthermore, what is the purpose of breathing? Is it just so we can have air flowing in and out of our body so we can claim the title of "alive," or is there a deeper purpose? Basic biology will teach us breathing is for the purpose of oxygenating our blood while expelling waste. This is required in both the born and the preborn. In the case of the preborn fetus, oxygen is provided to the child, not through air in the lungs, but across the placenta via the umbilical cord. This is the fetus' natural method of "breathing" without lungs. In both the born and the preborn, life-sustaining oxygen is supplied, and waste is expelled. The methodology may differ but neither is less human.

CONCLUSION

Life begins at conception and not at brain activity, first breath, or a heartbeat. My reasoning is plain. At the moment of conception, human DNA is created. These chains are the building blocks of human life.

While some claim that this is only basic cellular life, and not human, the cells are human cells. Furthermore, we are all just cellular life at varying stages of development. Since the cells are living and growing, and since uniquely human DNA exists, it stands to reason that these unique human lives. While a heartbeat does indeed provide evidence of life, it is not the only evidence. For instance, if the heart stops and then restarts aided by CPR, while we may say that the person died, it is not the case. He or she still had enough oxygen in their system to keep the cells alive until the heart could restart. This also goes hand in hand with the thought of breath determining life. I gave the example of the deep-sea free diver. If he does not allow enough time to resurface, he will drown. Thus, did he die when he took his last breath? I think we can all agree he died when he drowned. Again, so long as there are living cells and human DNA structure, how can it be said that human life has not begun?

Neither cell development, nor point of viability, nor geographical location determine human life, nor does the ability to breathe through the lungs. In each case, it serves as nothing more than evidence that the pro-choice community is not on the same page and is only grasping at straws in an effort to justify their selfish and wicked behavior. I am not saying that those who call themselves "pro-choice" are not fully convinced of their ideas but being convinced their reasoning is sound does not make it so. Neither sound logic nor sound reasoning allow for such desperate attempts to justify the killing of the preborn with impunity.

2.3 NOT A PERSON

Of all the arguments that have been brought up over the last 50 years, this one may be the most pertinent. As demonstrated, humanity is not up for discussion. Science just does not entertain the idea. Science cannot dictate or validate personhood. While everything else is chaff meant to get in the way, the legal argument is the linchpin that holds the pro-choice position together. If this pin can be successfully removed, the wheels will fall off the vehicle and their entire argument falls apart. Their argument ultimately rests on one major deficiency within our nation's laws.

U.S. Constitution, Preamble

We the People of the United States, in Order to form a more perfect Union, establish Justice, insure domestic Tranquility, provide for the common defence, promote the general Welfare, and secure the Blessings of Liberty to ourselves and our Posterity, do ordain and establish this Constitution for the United States of America.[xiv]

U.S. Constitution, Amendment XIV

All persons born or naturalized in the United States, and subject to the jurisdiction thereof, are citizens of the United States and of the State wherein they reside. No State shall make or enforce any law which shall abridge the privileges or immunities of citizens of the United States; nor shall any State deprive any person of life, liberty, or property, without due process of law; nor deny to any person within its jurisdiction the equal protection of the laws.[xv]

Our own Constitution, the very thing that recognizes our God-given inalienable rights and freedoms, is what is being used to justify the legal genocide of over 50 million children to date. The linchpin is a single word: person.

The preamble to the Constitution set the stage by declaring, "We the People," as those writing the document. Not only does it apply to the People but also to their posterity, or future generations. That begs the question: who exactly comprises their posterity? Science has already backed the humanity of the fetus. Sadly, as I stated earlier, it is incapable of determining personhood, as such a term is strictly legal in nature. Amendment XIV of the Constitution is where the terms are defined. It is this Amendment (and Amendment V) where it is declared that no person shall be deprived of life without due process of law. As it stands, our legal system only applies this to "all persons born or naturalized in the United States." Of course, we know this is not entirely true. This is why one cannot walk up to an illegal immigrant and shoot him on the spot. The immigrant is still afforded the basic right to life as the rest of us. The fetus, however, is not afforded the same title or right.

In 1973, the Supreme Court came to a decision regarding abortion. This decision was admittedly rooted in ignorance. The decision states, "We need not resolve the difficult question of when life begins. When those trained in the respective disciplines of medicine, philosophy, and theology are unable to arrive at any consensus, the judiciary, at this point in the development of man's knowledge, is not in a position to speculate as to the answer."[xvi] Common sense should dictate that where there is a lack of understanding, there should be an abundance of caution. Unfortunately, the highest court in our land threw all caution to the wind when it came to matters of when life began. While claiming to not have any way to know, they had already drawn a line in the sand by saying, "the word 'person,' as used in the Fourteenth Amendment, does not include the unborn."[xvii] For not having any way to definitively know when human life and personhood begins, they certainly did make a definitive declaration. This demonstrates nothing more than a tacit admission of making declarations in ignorance while handling human life with reckless abandon. Sadly, there have been catastrophic and lasting effects from this flawed and cowardly decision.

Pro-lifers make the logical assertion that, since the fetus is a human, and killing humans is immoral, abortion is immoral. However, pro-choicers take that same thought process and turn it on its head. Their claim can often be heard stating that since the Constitution declares it is immoral to kill a person, and the fetus is not considered a legal person, there is no immorality in destroying the fetus. Whether we like it or not, it is the same thought process and logic being utilized in an isolated sense. Dr. Willie Parker, an abortionist whose résumé boasts over 10,000 deaths by his own hands,[xviii] attempts to use this rationale to justify his occupation as an abortionist. Just as we desperately seek to correct pro-choicers when they claim the fetus is not a person, he tries to correct people who use the term "baby" to describe the fetus. In his book, *Life's Work*, he says, "But to refer to the fetus in utero as a baby is inaccurate. It reflects a hope, not a reality. In reference to a fetus, "baby" is a cultural term, not a scientific one."[xix] This is just the icing added to the cake of "it's not a person." While it is true that "baby" is a cultural term, terms do not define or dictate humanity. They only describe it. The irony is in his use of the term "fetus," as it is a Latin word that translates into "little one," or, in the case of humans, the vernacular of "small child" is fitting. What is a baby other than a small child? It would seem using baby is just as accurate as calling it a fetus. Contrary to the emotional ramblings within his book, the preborn are actual humans hoping to survive in a world shouting, "Crucify them!" But Dr. Parker is just the product of a worldview that denies the objective value of human life. It is one that says dignity is assigned rather than inherent. It is a worldview that sees the preborn as objects to be controlled rather than subjects to be respected and defended.[xx]

In defiance of all logic and common sense, under current law, the fetus is not a person until birth. It is only upon birth that all rights and privileges put forth in the Constitution apply. While it is inconsistent, it is now the legal precedent throughout the legal system. Just as pro-choice advocates have recognized this as the pivotal word, so have those of us who support life. The major push among many pro-life advocates and abolitionists is to have the law recognize the personhood of the preborn. It is to include them among the posterity of our founding fathers. If our nation will recognize the personhood of the preborn, it will ensure their lives cannot be deprived without due process within our legal system.[xxi] Until then, we will be left with a multitude of pro-choicers who adhere to the mindset that it is perfectly acceptable to kill humans so long as they are not killing persons. The wild acceptance of such a position should be enough to send chills down the spine of anyone capable of rational thought. Because of this widespread evil against the innocent, we must continue to fight with the understanding that, just because someone refuses to recognize the personhood of those whom she is oppressing our responsibility to help victims in their time of need is not alleviated.[xxii] Stand up for the preborn. Instead of viewing it as a burden or responsibility, it should be a joyful privilege to help the defenseless. After all, if persons are protected by law until the moment of death (which is the natural end), it stands to reason they should be protected from the moment of biological and natural beginning.[xxiii]

2.4 IT'S LEGAL

Until the personhood of the fetus is recognized and protected, the dehumanization of the preborn will continue, and abortion-on-demand will remain legal. Sadly, it is the very fact that it is legal that many choose to not even bother engaging in the discussion. For them, any attempt to discuss it is nothing more than being baited into justifying something that is their legal right. Legalities aside, we must always keep one question in mind: Do we have the moral right to do that which is morally wrong?[xxiv] While being wrong is never right, merely having the right does not always make us right.

Perhaps the strongest opposition to this argument is to be found in the example of slavery. Slavery used to be perfectly legal in our nation. Due to vague wording in the Constitution, coupled with the biased understanding of a racist society, blacks were not afforded the same rights and privileges as whites. In many ways, the problems black men, women, and children faced then are the same problems the preborn face today. Both were told they were not people. Both were considered less than human. Both could be killed. Both were considered the property of another. Neither were protected by the Constitution of the United States. This is less a deficiency in the Constitution and more indicative of a fallen and perverse society that has a long history of selfish and wicked agendas. At the hands of the government, these men and women were being denied their basic human rights. The government, however, is not the grantor of human rights. They can only choose to accept or reject what a person possesses by his or her very existence. Even though African Americans were denied the exercise of their rights, they could never be stripped of them before God. The idea of living in a society where the elected representatives can determine the legitimacy of a human right should scare everyone because, at this time, human rights are no longer rights. At such a point, they become human privileges that are granted (or rescinded) by the government as it sees fit.

While there are still many areas in which our nation needs to grow when it comes to racial tensions, on a societal level there are zero rights afforded to one ethnic group that are refused to another. In fact, we have a multitude of laws that prohibit such actions. It took many years, but we finally came around as a people and are continuing to refine ourselves. Today, if one were to reintroduce slavery as a viable economic practice, he would be shut down by an angry mob. The very concept is unthinkable by our society at large. My hope is the preborn will one day see the same level of support and abortion will be deemed an archaic practice from a past that needs to be learned from and never forgotten.

While I feel that should be enough to put the "It's Legal" argument to bed, I would like to bring up another particularly important example from our nation's not-so-distant history: *Buck v. Bell*. Proponents of abortion reject our charge that it is a human rights issue, while being quick to counter with the claim of it being a women's rights issue. Since abortion is legal, women can now maintain their rights. Given they are placing all stock in the legal status of abortion, I wonder how many of these advocates are aware of the outcome of *Buck v. Bell*, as it was a direct assault on the rights of Carrie Buck. The ruling upheld a 1924 decision that "the health of the patient and the welfare of society may be promoted in certain cases by the sterilization of mental defectives."[xxv]

Buck was the first woman to be sterilized under this law. While it was challenged to be a violation of the Fourteenth Amendment, in that it denied her due process of law,[xxvi] the Supreme Court affirmed the judgment of the 1924 decision,[xxvii] supporting their position with their experience showing "that heredity plays an important part in the transmission of insanity, imbecility, etc."[xxviii] Justice Oliver Wendell Holmes went so far as to say, "It is better for all the world if, instead of waiting to execute degenerate offspring for crime or to let them starve for their imbecility, society can prevent those who are manifestly unfit from continuing their kind," and followed it up with, "Three generations of imbeciles are enough."[xxix]

I love our justice system, but it is not perfect. This is a clear-cut case of violating the rights of both men and women in the name of eugenics. It should serve as evidence that, just because something is deemed legal, even at the highest court of the land, it does not automatically equate to being moral or right. We should be no freer to commit an act of eugenics in the forced sterilization of men and women based on their mental state than we should be free to commit an act of eugenics over the size, level of development, environment, or degree of dependency of another human being. If you support abortion because it is legal, ask yourself if you would have also supported the legal forced sterilization of Carrie Buck. After all, consistency is key.

2.5 UNWANTED

This is a surprisingly common objection despite its shallow nature. The claim is that a woman should not be forced to birth a baby she does not want. It is also backed by the claim that an unwanted child will be a burden to the mother and may grow up with a social and interpersonal difficulties.[xxx] However, I cannot think of a single viable reason why popularity or desire should dictate whether one deserves to live. Janet Morana makes an excellent point regarding the preborn when she says, "If they are 'wanted,' they are seen as a blessing, a miracle, a tiny bundle of unlimited potential. If they are unwanted, they are nothing but a parasite, a 'product of conception' that can be emptied from the unwilling mother's uterus. In reality, of course, a baby is a baby, wanted or otherwise."[xxxi]

There is no denying that it is always a sad state of affairs when a child is subjected to physical, mental, or emotional abuse. Some people, unfortunately, are not suited to be parents. Whether it be a child being kept inside a cage in a maggot-infested mobile home[xxxii] or some other equally as horrific headline, there is no shortage of depravity in this world. It is surprising that more people are not suffering from mental illness as our world falls apart before us.

This brings us back to the objection at hand. Is it truly an act of benevolent mercy to prevent potential suffering and psychological scarring by killing the child? Some pro-choicers think so. If that were so the case, would it not also be a benevolent act of mercy to execute children already living in such abuse? Why not end their misery? Where do we draw the line?

The answer should be obvious. There is no line to be drawn because the argument is fatally flawed from the start. The only way around it is to attempt to back it with one of the objections we have already reviewed. Of course, backing a fatally flawed argument with an equally flawed argument is contrary to sound reasoning. Ultimately, the only way out is to ignore the facts at hand, while sticking one's head in the sand. Instead of seeking to kill the sick and abused, we should find ways to help them. There are many ministries and resources assisting women and children who are struggling. This is far more loving than the alternative being presented by the pro-choice movement.

2.6 RAPE, INCEST, & GENETICS

Along with the objection that religion has no place in this discussion, making a case for exceptions due to rape and incest seems to be a favorite. This argument is employed, not only by the pro-choice movement but also by many who claim to be on the side of life. To be

24

fair, those who are deeply entrenched in the battle for preborn humanity do not typically cite such exemptions. They are cited by those who are ignorant of what they are saying. It is quite often this very objection that reveals whether someone is truly pro-life or if they are actually pro-choice but do not want to admit it. In my experience, this argument has become commonplace, not because it makes any logical sense, but because it is a highly emotional point. I am convinced the raw emotion of a sensitive topic and the commonality in hearing the exceptions being raised has resulted in so many who are willing to say they oppose abortion except in such cases.

RAPE

Similar to the argument of the baby being unwanted, this "special case" (i.e., rape) exception is also rooted in irrationality. However, instead of the latter being ascribed solely to the baby, the supposed concern is now for the mental health of the mother. Ironically enough, nobody is offering up the option to kill the pregnant rape victim as an act of benevolent mercy. Once again, the only option being presented is that which ends in the death of a child. Will the child potentially have psychological scarring from emotional abuse? Kill the baby! Will the mother potentially have psychological scarring from emotional and physical abuse? Kill the baby!

Just as not being wanted does not negate life, neither does the method of conception or the mental state of the mother. Both are valid concerns, but neither should result in the death of an innocent child. Sadly, just as our Constitution does not recognize the fetus as a person, neither does our judicial system. Because of this, the preborn can be slaughtered at the whim of the mother, with few restrictions. Instead of being protected by law, it allows for their death without a trial. The role of judge, jury, and executioner is wrapped up in one package called Mother.

To say a child conceived in rape is automatically worthy of death is to punish the child for the sins of the father. In many cases, it is to punish the child more severely than the rapist himself since rape is no longer a capital offense. In 1977, U.S. Supreme Court case, *Coker v. Georgia*, determined the death penalty was a violation of the Eighth Amendment in that it was considered too harsh a punishment for the crime committed.[xxxiii] Yet, the child conceived in rape can be readily subjected to such punishment. Thus, recognizing the personhood of the preborn is critical.

I would be remiss to think a rape victim would not be traumatized by being reminded of it daily as she sees her belly grow. I cannot even imagine the potential horror that would exist if the baby ended up inheriting the facial features of his or her father. Instead of seeing a bouncing bundle of joy, you see your rapist every time you look at your child. There are some who choose to keep their child, of course, and cannot fathom having an abortion after being raped. But that does not mean all mothers are as resilient. As with all challenges and tragedies, some people are affected more than others. Some may need additional help to overcome the trauma of rape.

But murdering her child just is neither therapeutic, nor a viable option to help her move forward. All it does is add insult to injury. It transforms the victim into the assailant. While on the road to recovery after being assaulted, she becomes a murderer, opting to send her own child down a path in which recovery is not an option. To recover some semblance of hope, she first removes all hope from her baby. We do not cure victims by turning them into murderers…from being preyed upon to becoming a predator. As Janet Morana has said, "Abortion does not 'cure' rape. It merely answers one evil with another evil. Rape is a grave injustice, but killing an innocent child is also a grave injustice."[xxxiv]

INCEST

When you hear the exceptions for rape, you are likely to hear incest alongside it. The two seem to be joined at the hip as if they belong together. While incest may occur through rape, it can also be voluntary. The primary argument made in this objection is that the child is more likely to be born with a severe birth defect or mental deficiency. Statistics show that a child born from a first-degree incestuous relationship is at up to a 50% greater health risk than other babies.[xxxv]

This is a significant statistic that should be taken seriously, but it should hold no weight in determining whether a child should be killed. Furthermore, while we are on the subject of statistics, both rape and incest are rarely cited as reasons for choosing abortion. Only 1% of all abortions are due to rape, and less than half of a percent are due to incest.[xxxvi] For being such a common argument, one would think the numbers would be higher. If anything, this shows that just because an argument is frequently stated, it does not make it valid.

GENETIC DEFECTS

This is an area that has become taboo. With our culture of inclusivity, we have seen those with Down syndrome being represented at unprecedented rates in everything from modeling to activism. A plethora of organizations exist to promote awareness for the condition while seeking to educate the masses on a topic most are largely ignorant on. On average there are roughly 6,000 children with Down syndrome born every year.[xxxvii] Statistics show that 67% of parents opt to have an abortion once the fetus is diagnosed with the syndrome.[xxxviii]

That makes thousands of children who are murdered every year solely because they were not typical in the physical sense. Because they possessed a slightly different chromosomal makeup, they were automatically deemed inferior and not deserving of life. But what of those who are alive today with Down syndrome? Are they not deserving of life? Are they still a burden to society and a danger to themselves? Of course not! I have a friend whose son has Down syndrome and he is an awesome kid! This is why the organizations mentioned above are so important. Having a child with Down syndrome, while possessing unique challenges, should not be a death sentence. As a parent, I think it is natural for us to hope and pray our children will be healthy, but that does not mean we should stop loving them just because we learn they have health concerns. Whether it be an additional chromosome (Down syndrome),[xxxix] a missing chromosome (Turner syndrome),[xl] or any other form of genetic variation, we need to embrace the differences within mankind all the way down to the genetic level. Stop dehumanizing people just because they are unique.

2.7 I CAN'T AFFORD A BABY!

With this poverty claim comes the charge that the pro-life community is irresponsible, loveless, and merely pro-birth, as opposed to pro-life. This is yet another desperate attempt to ignore the wicked foundation of the pro-choice platform while adopting the same "holier than thou" mentality so many in the camp openly condemn. However, as is commonplace in a community of wickedness, it is only condemned when it threatens their sanctuary of guilt-free living.

The basis for this claim is that a child should not be brought into this world unless the mother can financially provide for him or her. We see this taking place across the board, not just when it comes to matters of abortion. More than ever before, men and women are delaying having children to focus on their careers and financial stability first. On average, women are now waiting until age 26 before having children, vice the previous age of 21. Men are typically waiting until age 31, vice 27.[xli] For the purposes of this book, I will not be going into their reasons for doing so. When families opt to wait, that is between the husband and wife. Ultimately, raising children is expensive. As a father of three, I know how much it costs, and I am bracing for the impact of the "driving years" yet to come. Studies have shown the typical middle-income family will spend nearly $13,000 per child annually.[xlii] This is nothing to sneeze at! That said, is this a noble argument or only a talking point in the topic of abortion?

If I decide I can no longer afford to feed my dog, and I decide to shoot her in the skull, am I making a smart financial decision, or am I a money-hungry monster with zero regard for innocent life? I think we can all agree I would be hounded (pun intended), not only by PETA, but also by just about anyone with even an ounce of compassion, and rightfully so! If only the same standard would be applied to the preborn. Money and financial stability can lend to higher quality of life, but it should never lead to the termination of life. Like it or not, under our current laws, every human life hangs in the balance of its mother's choice. She is legally authorized to choose whether to allow her child to continue living (though they may struggle financially) or kill her child in an attempt to obtain financial freedom.

Regarding the charge that pro-lifers are only pro-birth, one does not need to adopt every child to have a genuine care for their right to live. To make an analogy, picture a group of teens running around a city's streets killing all its homeless people. When asked why they were doing it, imagine them claiming they were acts of benevolent mercy. After all, those homeless people were living in extreme temperatures, had no access to healthcare, and had to beg for food. Would you not find such a reasoning horrendous? Nearly everyone seems more than willing to share their thoughts in the comments section of any given news story these days. Would you be in the comments condemning those who speak out against the teens? Would your comments accuse them of being only anti-killing and not actually anti-homeless since they aren't willing to house the homeless and singlehandedly solve the problem of homelessness? Certainly, such an idea would be mocked by many, and it sounds ridiculous even as I type it. Yet, this is the same argumentation used by those who charge pro-lifers with being merely pro-birth, or anti-abortion, and not actually pro-life. But one need not be capable of resolving the problem of evil to recognize it exists and speak against it. Additionally, just as the other previously addressed arguments are strawmen, this one is no exception. The pro-life community is very sensitive to the needs and desires within the heart and mind of a woman carrying her unexpected child.

There are many thoughts racing through the mother's mind as she ponders her situation. On the one hand, she may believe her child is nothing but a clump of cells. Thus, it becomes more a matter of whether to try out this new potential thing called a child. Of course, this argument has already been addressed above. On the other hand, many mothers are likely afraid. They are afraid of being ostracized. They are afraid of not being able to go to college. They are afraid of not being able to buy food. They are afraid of not being able to pay their rent. All of these are valid concerns, amplified by a lack of education and training regarding existing assistance and resources.

But there are many programs available to help expectant and new mothers. Programs like the Special Supplemental Nutrition Program for Women, Infants, and Children (WIC) help offset the cost of raising young children by providing vouchers for groceries, and healthcare referrals. Women can remain enrolled so long as they are breastfeeding, and children can be enrolled until the age of five.[xliii] This is a tremendous support for families who are unable to afford groceries. For health coverage, there are government programs such as Medicaid and Children's Health Insurance Program (CHIP). These programs help a vast number of low-income families, ensuring that health is not being sacrificed. CHIP assists children up until age 19, subject to qualification.[xliv]

Another available resource is your local Crisis Pregnancy Center (CPC). These facilities exist to give hope to pregnant women who might be pondering an abortion. They provide ultrasounds, testing for sexually transmitted diseases, counseling, and maternity clothing. There are currently thousands of CPCs across the nation waiting to help pregnant women overcome the obstacles facing them. Unfortunately, CPCs have recently come under attack. Pro-choice activists have targeted them for harassment. A quick online search will produce numerous results demonstrating this. The reason they are so targeted is because they do not offer or recommend abortion. That would be antithetical to their morals. For them, abortion is not an option.

Because of this, their opponents accuse them of being shady and deceptive. They are accused of withholding the option of abortion while shaming the mother into keeping her child. A Crisis Pregnancy Center located near me was vandalized in 2019 when a window was shattered with a rock and the walls were spray-painted with words and phrases such as 'Fake,' 'You Hate Women,' and an array of vulgarity.[xlv] The only reason for such anger and hatred is because the opposition feels threatened. I encourage you to reach out to your local CPC and see how you can support them or lend a hand.

In the end, some women may still feel overwhelmed at the prospect of having a baby. Is all hope lost at this point? Have we reached the point where abortion is finally the only viable conclusion? Of course not! There is still one particularly important option remaining on the table: adoption. Someone close to me chose this option after having gone through an earlier abortion. She lives with the constant guilt of having murdered her child. That guilt prevented her from going through with another. But she also knew there was no way she could afford another child, as she was already struggling to make ends meet for her and her daughter. I am happy to report that, despite living in a world trying to convince her that another abortion was the right move, she listened to her conscience. She made the extremely difficult decision to carry her baby to term, and then gave him away to another family. During her pregnancy, the adopting family paid for all related expenses as they eagerly awaited the chance to welcome a baby into their loving home. Today, her son is living an incredibly happy life with parents who love him very much. This brave woman told me she has no regrets and knows she made the right decision.

The above are only some of the resources available to new or pregnant mothers. The point is that pregnant women are not alone. There are literally thousands of organizations out there ready to lend a helping hand, and many childless parents seeking a child to adopt. Sadly, many abortion advocates continually seek to silence such help as it is a direct threat to their murdering industry.

2.8 BETTER THAN COAT HANGERS

Oftentimes, pro-choice advocates like to use scare tactics as an attempt to keep abortion legal. One such tactic is in getting people to believe that, if abortion were to be made illegal, pregnant women would turn back to the use of coat hangers to perform self-induced abortions. The common term is "back-alley abortion," painting a grim picture of unsanitary and dangerous conditions where the mother is likely to die as a victim of violence. However, instead of being mugged, the woman is forced to die alone at the hands of pro-life activists who refused her the proper medical care she deserved.

I would like to address this last point first and then work back from there. Is abortion-on-demand a medical procedure? The goal of medicine is to preserve or restore health. This can be both preventative and corrective. But is that what abortion-on-demand accomplishes? Many argue that abortion is a medical procedure that must be readily accessible for the health of women. But is maternal death really so common that it warrants the legal killing of another human being?

Based on the numbers provided by the CDC, in 2009, there were around 6,369,000 pregnancies in the United States.[xlvi] Of this total, the number of maternal deaths was 734.[xlvii] Keep in mind, this figure is not only those who died during pregnancy, but also factored from complications that arose post-partum when the baby was already alive and protected by law. Thus, the following figure is actually on the significantly high side if we were to only consider deaths during pregnancy itself. Mathematically, the maternal death rate for 2009 was 0.0001152%. That is an incredibly small percentage to be using for a mainstream argument and considered an epidemic, justifying the murder of nearly 1,000,000 preborn humans every year, all in the name of choice.

Unfortunately, even with such statistics, many try to sell it as if maternal deaths were widespread and commonplace. If I told you that you had a 0.0001152% chance of being killed in a car accident on your next drive, I imagine you would consider that to be hardly worth taking into account when it came to your decision to drive or stay home. This is further amplified by the fact that, in abortion, a woman is saying she should raise the death toll of her baby to a 100% chance to avoid her 0.0001152% chance. The reality is that, even as low as the numbers are, the majority of all abortions are not to avoid a 0.0001152% chance of risk but are actually a matter of convenience.

I stand with Philip Ney in his assessment that "women choosing to have an abortion are not patients because: pregnancy is not an illness, their choice is not an indication for treatment, their distress is not a disease."[xlviii] Pregnancy is a natural state, not a disease, adverse genetic mutation, or any other illness. Words have meaning.

Not only does abortion not fit in the definition of medicine, the Hippocratic Oath (the oath taken by all doctors) is avidly opposed to abortion. It states, "I will not give a lethal drug to anyone if I am asked, nor will I advise such a plan; and similarly I will not give a woman a pessary to cause an abortion."[xlix] The very oath sworn by all doctors, albeit nonbinding in a legal sense, puts abortion in the same paragraph as killing a person via a lethal drug prescription. The very basis of modern medicine rejects abortion as being antithetical to medical practice.

Going back into the alley, we must ask ourselves how much truth there is to the claim. Is it descriptive of an archaic period from not so long ago, or is it a lie meant to prey on the emotions of vulnerable young women? For the sake of argument, let us first assume it is a valid claim. What if outlawing abortion would lead to a massive spike in deaths from illegal abortions via coat hangers? Would this be enough to change your mind to be in favor of pro-choice?

Very few function under the assumption that the law has little to no effect on the actions of humanity. I would argue it has great effect. It is only because of the law, and its binding consequences, that humanity does not slip even further into depravity than it already has.

Personally, I enjoy the thrill of speed. However, I taper back on the throttle because I don't find the threat of a speeding ticket or jail to be very exhilarating. Similarly, most thieves don't rob houses in broad daylight or in front of a police station. For that matter, when my own children would act out of line, it often only took me speaking in a firm tone before they would fall in line. They knew the consequences of their actions if they continued. At every level of society, from the rules of the home to the rules of the State, laws are largely effective at keeping the people in check. Even abortionists have admitted that, though they believe abortion restrictions violate human freedom, they obey them for fear they will be shut down if caught breaking them.[i] Succinctly stated: laws work!

Yes, there will always be criminals. There are those who, in spite of consequences, will do what they want. As children, we grow up learning we can do whatever we want, but those actions will always have consequences, whether good or bad. Knowing there are thieves, should we abolish anti-theft laws and make stealing legal? Since we know there are murderers, should murder be decriminalized and all instances of it be removed from our penal code (much like New York did with terminology of abortion)?

History and statistics should help paint a clearer picture. Just look up annual abortion statistics within the first decade after abortion was made legal. The numbers skyrocketed, with each year building on the previous. If nothing else, this is evidence that the legalization of abortion caused people to come out of the woodwork in record numbers. In fact, from 1973 to 1981, the number of abortions performed in the U.S. had doubled[ii] to 1.3 million![iii] Clearly, the illegal nature of abortion had curbed the actions of the general population.

So, what do we make of the largescale numbers that were being claimed by the pro-choice movement just prior to abortion being declared legal? According to those metrics, there were nearly 1,000,000 women having illegal abortions performed and roughly 10,000 women were dying every year because of unsanitary conditions, many from bleeding out after performing a self-induced abortion with a coat hanger. Earlier, I accepted this talking point only as a matter of setting the stage. In reality, their claim was a lie from the beginning and had absolutely zero substance to it.

Dr. Bernard Nathanson, co-founder of NARAL Pro-Choice America, has come clean in multiple interviews over the years. He has been quoted as admitting:

> We persuaded the media that the cause of permissive abortion was a liberal enlightened, sophisticated one. Knowing that if a true poll were taken, we would be soundly defeated, we simply fabricated the results of fictional polls. We announced to the media that we had taken polls and that 60 percent of Americans were in favor of permissive abortion. This is the tactic of the self-fulfilling lie. Few people care to be in the minority...We aroused enough sympathy to sell our program of permissive abortion by fabricating the number of illegal abortions done annually in the U.S. The actual figure was approaching 100,000 but the figure we gave to the media repeatedly was 1,000,000...The number of women dying from illegal abortions was around 200-250 annually. The figure we constantly fed to the media was 10,000,"[liii]

and,

> "I confess that I knew the figures were totally false, and I suppose the others did too if they stopped to think of it. But in the 'morality' of our revolution, it was a useful figure, widely accepted, so why go out of our way to correct it with honest statistics? The overriding concern was to get the laws eliminated, and anything within reason that had to be done was permissible."[liv]

This should insult anyone who bought into their lie. An entire worldview was fabricated out of deception, rooted in nothing more than a desire to see an agenda come to fruition. The ends justified the means, even if it meant lying to the nation and manipulating the populace through emotional deception and abuse. Much like today's Leftist agenda, the media was used to indoctrinate the people. Let history serve as a glaring reminder that wickedness knows no bounds, and the tactics employed will use whatever medium might efficiently spread the message.

Horror stories of women bleeding out, with coat hanger in hand, may have been widespread, but it was anything but true. The fact of the matter was that most abortions were performed in sanitary conditions by licensed medical professionals who were in violation of both the law and their sworn oath. Instead of 10,000 women dying per year, it was in the realm of 200-250, with an overall death rate of 0.25%. Yet, even as late as 1996, there were still people on the fence due to moral uncertainty. This was when President Bill Clinton coined the phrase, "Safe, Legal, and Rare," in an attempt to win people over.[lv] After all, if it is safe, legal, and rare, it can't be all that bad, right? Sadly, time has shown how flawed that phrase really proved to be. While promised a safe procedure, roughly 205 women have died as a direct result of a legal abortion procedure,[lvi] and we have gone from 100,000 abortions per year to 862,000 in 2017.[lvii] That is an increase of over 800% for something touted as rare. However, even if zero mothers were harmed during the procedure, an innocent human life is taken every time. Truly, abortion has nothing to do with healthcare, and is only self-care at the irreversible expense of another.

2.9 MY BODY, MY CHOICE!

Undoubtedly, this is the number one argument that far surpasses all others. Whether it be in the form of, "No Uterus, No Opinion," "My Body, My Choice," or any host of other quips, they all imply a woman has the right to do what she wants with her own body.

To a certain extent, I would agree. Nobody is trying to tell her how she is to cut her hair. Nobody is trying to tell her she cannot get a tattoo, sleep with as many partners as she pleases, or reserve herself for only one person. No, all of these are her rights and nobody can strip her of them. Yet, they all fail to recognize one critical factor: there are, at a minimum, two bodies at play in the equation.

Some will argue the fetus is only an extension of the mother's body. The idea is that the mother should have full reign over her body and anything that is a part of it. However, this just does not make any sense. In order for that to be the case, the mother now has two hearts, four lungs, ten fingers, ten toes, two different blood types, and ninety-two chromosomes that make up two distinct genomes. While the mother is certainly carrying the fetus, it is no more an extension of her body than the father was at the moment of conception. Furthermore, going back to the previously used example of conjoined twins, it doesn't get much more connected than that. In fact, in the case of conjoined twins, they are even more connected than the mother and her preborn child. In pregnancy, the child is living within the mother while being a distinct body with distinct organs. In cases of conjoined twins, two distinct people are actually sharing certain organs. Does this give one the right to kill the other after staking claim to said organs? Being physically joined does not automatically equate to being an extension with ownership rights. This position throws another monkey wrench into the equation when taken to its fullest extent. As David Hershenov has pointed out, "If killing innocents were permissible only when they are parts, then newborns could be killed prior to the cutting of the umbilical cord, while embryos not yet embedded in the uterine wall could not be terminated. Oddly, abortifacients would be immoral but infanticide would not."[lviii]

Sadly, that is exactly how the fetus is viewed in many cases. It becomes a matter of ownership and property. The unique person is, at best, marginalized, and, at worst, dehumanized. It is maddening that women would fight so hard for equality, only to treat the little women in their womb as property. The literal stripping of humanity and deprivation of personhood from women in their most vulnerable state has become a staple in the fight for women's rights. It truly is a tragic irony of a degenerate worldview.

As I alluded to earlier, abortion really is just the latest form of slavery. After all, slavery was once a legal, lucrative business practice where men and women were robbed of their humanity and personhood, only to be treated as property with nobody being qualified to tell the master he was wrong to do as he pleased with his own property. Instead of breaking away from a wicked act of our past, it seems society has chosen to borrow from the fundamentals and apply it to something that will not fight back. As another dose of tragic irony, while the black community makes up only 13 percent of our nation's population,[lix] 28 percent of all abortions come from it.[lx] This is just another example of adding insult to injury, as the people group that was most impacted by the atrocities of slavery is the same group that is treating other people as property at a highly disproportionate rate.

But isn't this about what women want? After all, even if it is conceded that the preborn is a unique human life known by God, isn't the mother's body the more important one at the moment? How do we address challenges and claims such as this? Is it a valid point or is it just another form of lording superiority over another?

First of all, we need to address the idea that an abortion is what the mother wants. As Frederica Matthewes-Green has pointed out, "No one wants an abortion as she wants an ice cream or a Porsche. She wants an abortion as an animal, caught in a trap, wants to gnaw off its own leg."[lxi] The imagery is that of a scared animal desperately trying to be free even at the expense of great physical and emotional trauma. While serial abortionists exist, those cases are most often comprised of women who neither take pleasure nor show remorse and feel it is a valid alternative to pregnancy. One would be hard pressed to find normative examples of women who seek pregnancy just so they can have an abortion, as some kind of rush of endorphins. Thus, wants are not really a factor here as much as a feeling of necessity or desiring to maintain freedom of choice.

Second, we need to see if there is a precedent for limitations of our freedoms when it comes to encounters between two unique human beings. One common theory is that of the Non-Aggression Principle (NAP). The basic tenet of this theory is that a person does not possess the right to hurt another unless in defense of an act of aggression. While there have been many advocates and opponents to this principle, the core understanding is actually in line with many of our societal laws. This is why I am free to wave my arms erratically, but I am not free to wave them erratically into someone's face. A person is free to have consensual sex with a partner, but that same person is not free to rape said partner. Likewise, a woman is free to do as she pleases with her body, but she is not free to harm the body of another. The location of the other body does not negate the existence of a unique person who has done no harm nor committed an act of aggression.

Yet, despite this, such a logical mindset is still viewed as being bound by the patriarchy. It concludes that a lack of freedom equates to oppression. In that case, it all depends how one defines oppression. If you define it as someone limiting your free actions in any way whatsoever, I would agree in full. Police officers are oppressing her. Lawmakers are oppressing her. In this case, any removal of choice without consequence would be defined as oppression. However, most would agree this is a necessary oppression to prevent us, as a society, from slipping into chaos and anarchy. Because of this differentiation, we must limit the definition of oppression to simply the limiting of one's rights. Does one have the right to take the life of another? Countless court verdicts shout a resounding no.

How can a woman possibly imply her rights are being violated if the only limitation is her ability to destroy the unborn child within her womb? This is not a violation of rights. This is not oppression. In fact,

I truly believe one of the greatest tragedies of the modern era is people being convinced it is right for a mother to be able to kill her child, and being told "no" is oppressive. Referencing an above argument, it is why it is critical that the personhood of the unborn be recognized. Rights are imbued to us all as human beings regardless of our age. As for the right to life, there is zero justification for taking it away without due process in a court of law. Since the preborn has committed no crime, any charges against him or her should be instantly dismissed. There is no case. Court adjourned!

Going back to the "No Uterus, No Opinion" quip mentioned earlier, think about what that really entails. If men were disqualified from making decisions that affected a woman's body, abortion would still be against the law. Think about that long and hard. Who was it that occupied the Supreme Court on January 22, 1973 when *Roe v. Wade* was settled? It was a court of nine males. There was not a single female in the lot. Where were all the protests on January 23rd in an effort to fight against the injustice of men making decisions on behalf of women? Let us not forget that it was also a group of men who declared the 19th Amendment, recognizing a woman's right to vote, to be Constitutional. Based on the evidence presented, it appears the pro-choice crowd really doesn't care about whether or not one has a uterus, so long as the opinion matches their own. The signs would be more accurate is they read, "No Uterus, No Dissenting Opinion." Yet, even then, such quips fail to take into account the large numbers of women who continually fight for the rights of the preborn. In these cases, the signs would be more accurate if they read, "Don't You Dare Disagree with Me or I'll Be Forced to Create an Illogical and Inconsistent Quip." Yes, I know, it is a bit wordy. Better to sound trendy, even if illogical, than to be logical and get laughed at, I suppose.

What should be abundantly clear by now is that it is not about a woman's ability to do as she pleases with her own body. It is about a woman's inability to do as she pleases to the body of another. Once she becomes pregnant, it is no longer about her body. This is just one of many red herrings meant to draw the attention away from the actual issue. Sarah Quale says it best, "The battle is no longer pro-life versus pro-choice; it's woman versus fetus."[lxii] Though, under our current laws, she may have the right to an abortion, we must always ask ourselves if simply having a right is synonymous with doing what is right.

Even after all the facts are laid out, there are still many who hold to inconsistent views. Time and again, I have run into people who claim abortion is wrong, and they would never have one, but they also do not feel it is their place to make that decision for another person. I always ask such people why they feel this way. I ask because I am genuinely curious of their answer. More often than not, it is because they feel choice should not be infringed upon. I then ask if they believe a person should have the right to kill my children. The answer is always an emphatic, "No!" I then ask why they are pro-life. This answer is less consistent, but usually involves some form of sympathy for the unborn child. I then wrap it up by asking how the unborn child being killed freely by the mother is any different than my child being killed freely by another. This position is one of touting kindness to others while, at the same time, saying a person should be free to commit an irreversible act of violence toward another in the most reprehensible of ways, all in the name of preserving free will. If one truly understands the validity of the life inside the mother, no amount of freedom will justify completing this sentence: "It is okay to brutally murder a child when _____."

---

[i] Frank A. Pavone, *Abolishing Abortion: How You Can Play a Part in Ending the Greatest Evil of Our Day* [Nashville: Nelson Books, 2015], 17-18

[ii] Janet Morana, *Recall Abortion* [Charlotte: Saint Benedict Press, 2013],57

[iii] Ken Ham, *A Pocket Guide to Social Issues: Are There Really Different Races?* [Petersburg: Answers in Genesis, 2009], 53

[iv] Peter Barnes, *Abortion: Open Your Mouth for the Dumb* [East Peoria: The Banner of Truth Trust, 2010], 11

[v] Tommy Mitchell, *A Pocket Guide to Social Issues: When Does Life Begin?* [Petersburg: Answers in Genesis, 2009], 22

[vi] Ibid., 11

[vii] Peter Barnes, *Abortion: Open Your Mouth for the Dumb* [East Peoria: The Banner of Truth Trust, 2010], 14

[viii] Tommy Mitchell, *A Pocket Guide to Social Issues: When Does Life Begin?* [Petersburg: Answers in Genesis, 2009], 13

[ix] Ibid, pg. 12

[x] A recent headline demonstrated this fact. A 15-month-old baby died of starvation and dehydration after the mother died of an overdose. The child was strapped in a child car seat and died after three days of being unattended. This is a tragedy, not an excuse to kill the child because he was only 'viable' for three days without direct care, intervention, and support of the mother. WBIR Staff, "Tennessee toddler starved to death after mom overdosed, autopsy shows," *13News Now*, June 15, 2021, https://www.13newsnow.com/article/news/crime/tennessee-toddler-starved-to-death-mom-overdosed/51-449c1ebc-ae3e-4b4e-85d0-ae2d6b377b8d

[xi] Sarah Seaton, et al., *Babies born at the threshold of viability: changes in survival and workload over 20 years*. Archives of disease in childhood, Fetal and neonatal edition, 98(1), 2013: F15–F20, https://doi.org/10.1136/fetalneonatal-2011-301572

[xii] Ashley May, "Mom pleads with doctor to resuscitate baby delivered at 21 weeks. 'Miracle' daughter is now a toddler," *USA Today*, November 14, 2017, https://www.usatoday.com/story/news/nation-now/2017/11/14/mom-delivers-earliest-premature-baby-ever-and-chooses-resuscitate-miracle-aughter-now-healthy-toddle/861386001/

[xiii] Tommy Mitchell, *A Pocket Guide to Social Issues: When Does Life Begin?* [Petersburg: Answers in Genesis, 2009], 15

[xiv] U.S. Const. pmbl

[xv] U.S. Const. amend. XIV

[xvi] Roe v. Wade, 410 U.S. 113, 159 (1973)

[xvii] Roe v. Wade, 410 U.S. 113, 158 (1973)

[xviii] Willie Parker, *Life's Work: A Moral Argument for Choice* [New York: Simon & Schuster, 2017], 143

[xix] Ibid., 155

[xx] Daniel C. Becker, *Personhood The Tree of Life: The Biblical Path to Pro-Life Victory in the 21st Century* [Alpharetta: Personhood, 2017], 3

[xxi] Gregory J. Roden, *Issues in Law & medicine*. 2010 Spring; 25(3): 185-273

[xxii] Frank A. Pavone, *Abolishing Abortion: How You Can Play a Part in Ending the Greatest Evil of Our Day* [Nashville: Nelson Books, 2015], 48

[xxiii] Daniel C. Becker, *Personhood The Tree of Life: The Biblical Path to Pro-Life Victory in the 21st Century* [Alpharetta: Personhood, 2017], 5

[xxiv] R.C. Sproul, *Abortion: A Rational Look at an Emotional Issue* [Lake Mary: Reformation Trust Publishing, 2010], 115

[xxv] Buck v. Bell, 274 U.S. 205 (1927)

[xxvi] ibid.

[xxvii] Buck v. Bell, 274 U.S. 208 (1927)

[xxviii] Buck v. Bell, 274 U.S. 206 (1927)

[xxix] Buck v. Bell, 274 U.S. 207 (1927)

[xxx] Aníbal Faúndes & José Barzelatto, *The Human Drama of Abortion: A Global Search for Consensus* [United Kingdom: Vanderbilt University Press, 2006], 39

[xxxi] Janet Morana, *Recall Abortion* [Charlotte: Saint Benedict Press, 2013], 56

[xxxii] Laken Bowles & Rebekah Hammonds, *Toddler Found in Cage in Henry County*, https://www.newschannel5.com/news/toddler-found-in-a-cage-during-henry-co-animal-rescue

[xxxiii] Coker v. Georgia, 433 U.S. 584 (1977)

[xxxiv] Janet Morana, *Recall Abortion* [Charlotte: Saint Benedict Press, 2013], 95

[xxxv] Hal Herzog, *The Problem with Incest. Evolution, morality, and the politics of abortion.* https://www.psychologytoday.com/us/blog/animals-and-us/201210/the-problem-incest

[xxxvi] Lawrence Finer, et al., *Reasons U.S. women have abortions: quantitative and qualitative perspectives. Perspectives on sexual and reproductive health*, 37(3), 2005: 110–118, https://www.guttmacher.org/journals/psrh/2005/reasons-us-women-have-abortions-quantitative-and-qualitative-perspectives

[xxxvii] National Down Syndrome Society, *What is Down Syndrome?* https://www.ndss.org/about-down-syndrome/down-syndrome/

[xxxviii] Chris Kaposy, "The Ethical Case for Having a Baby With Down Syndrome," *New York Times*, April 16, 2018, https://www.nytimes.com/2018/04/16/opinion/down-syndrome-abortion.html

[xxxix] Centers for Disease Control, *Facts About Down Syndrome*, https://www.cdc.gov/ncbddd/birthdefects/downsyndrome.html

[xl] MedlinePlus, Bethesda (MD): National Library of Medicine (US), *Turner syndrome*, https://medlineplus.gov/genetics/condition/turner-syndrome/

[xli] Ashley Stahl, "New Study: Millennial Women Are Delaying Having Children Due To Their Careers," *Forbes*, May 1, 2020, https://www.forbes.com/sites/ashleystahl/2020/05/01/new-study-millennial-women-are-delaying-having-children-due-to-their-careers/#45cde7fa276a

[xlii] Mark Lino, "The Cost of Raising a Child," *U.S. Department of Agriculture*, January 13, 2017, https://www.usda.gov/media/blog/2017/01/13/cost-raising-child

[xliii] https://www.fns.usda.gov/wic

[xliv] https://www.usa.gov/benefits

[xlv] Martin Weil, "Vandalism reported at Christian pregnancy center in central Va.," *The Washington Post*, February 2, 2019, https://www.washingtonpost.com/local/public-safety/vandalism-reported-at-

christian-pregnancy-center-in-central-va/2019/02/02/50bf4754-26a7-11e9-ad53-824486280311_story.html

xlvi Centers for Disease Control, *Pregnancy Rates for U.S. Women Continue to Drop*, https://www.cdc.gov/nchs/products/databriefs/db136.htm

xlvii Centers for Disease Control, *Pregnancy Mortality Surveillance System*, https://www.cdc.gov/reproductivehealth/maternal-mortality/pregnancy-mortality-surveillance-system.htm

xlviii Philip Ney, "Abortion, Conscience Clauses, and the Practice of Medicine," *LifeNews*, December 2, 2010, http://lifenews.com/2010/12/02/opi-1025/

xlix Michael North, National Library of Medicine: *Greek Medicine*. https://www.nlm.nih.gov/hmd/greek/greek_oath.html

l Willie Parker, *Life's Work: A Moral Argument for Choice* [New York: Simon & Schuster, 2017], 10

li Guttmacher Institute, *Induced Abortions in the United States*, https://www.guttmacher.org/fact-sheet/induced-abortion-united-states

lii Centers for Disease Control, *Current Trends Abortion Surveillance: Preliminary Analysis -- United States, 1981*, https://www.cdc.gov/mmwr/preview/mmwrhtml/00000366.htm

liii Bernard Nathanson, ", Pro-choice co-founder rips abortion industry," *World Net Daily*, December 2002, http://www.wnd.com/2002/12/16344

liv Bernard Nathanson, *Aborting America* [New York: Pinnacle Books, 1979], 193

lv Lainey Newman, *Harvard Political Review, Safe, Legal, and Rare: The Democrats' Evolving Stance on Abortion*, Jan 11, 2018, https://harvardpolitics.com/united-states/safe-legal-and-rare-the-democrats-evolving-stance-on-abortion/

lvi Centers for Disease Control, *Data and Statistics*, https://www.cdc.gov/reproductivehealth/data_stats/index.htm

lvii Guttmacher Institute, *The U.S. Abortion Rate Continues to Drop: Once Again, State Abortion Restrictions Are Not the Main Driver*, https://www.guttmacher.org/gpr/2019/09/us-abortion-rate-continues-drop-once-again-state-abortion-restrictions-are-not-main

[lviii] David Hershenov, *Public Discourse. Ten (Bad, But Popular) Arguments for Abortion*, August 23, 2017. https://www.thepublicdiscourse.com/2017/08/19718/

[lix] United States Census Bureau, *Quick Facts – United States*, https://www.census.gov/quickfacts/fact/table/US/PST045219

[lx] Guttmacher Institute, *U.S. Abortion Patients*, https://www.guttmacher.org/infographic/2016/us-abortion-patients

[lxi] Frederica Matthewes-Green, *Real Choices: Listening to Women, Looking for Alternatives to Abortion* [Chesterton: Conciliar Press, 1997]

[lxii] Daniel C. Becker, *Personhood The Tree of Life: The Biblical Path to Pro-Life Victory in the 21st Century* [Alpharetta: Personhood, 2017], 49

3 PRO-LIFE, ABOLITION, & THEONOMY

Pro-life, pro-choice, or other? There was a time when I thought the first two were the only major camps. Sure, there were always variations of people within each camp but, by and large, most people fell into one of the two. However, there is another camp that falls somewhere else entirely. This particular camp shares similarities with the religious zealots of biblical times. For those who may be unaware, the zealots were those who were religious fanatics to the point where they would murder the opposing government officials. One could consider them religious assassins. While this third category is not necessarily out bombing abortion clinics (nor would they advocate such tactics), their extremism is performed in a very different, yet equally as dangerous, manner. So who is this mystery category? It contains those deemed as abolitionists. The most prominent organizations in this category are Abolish Human Abortion (AHA) and End Abortion Now (EAN). For the purposes of this chapter, I would like to focus on the former as it was the group that primed the abolitionist movement.

AHA members come in a variety of shapes and sizes but they all have one thing in common: abolishing abortion. On this particular point, I have no disagreement. As Christians, the complete eradication of evil should always be strived for. However, we must also understand we live in a fallen world with unregenerate sinners. Thus, it should be understood that, this side of heaven, we will never achieve that end goal. AHA is an interesting group as it neither falls under pro-life nor pro-choice. In fact, they will openly proclaim that both movements entertain evil and are wicked. Not so long ago, I would have been scratching my head asking myself what else is left. Now, it is not quite as confusing. My end conclusion? AHA is both misguided as well as dangerous.

When I first heard of AHA, I decided to follow them on Facebook and even shared some of their posts. Imagine my surprise when I heard they were picketing churches and protesting bills that directly attacked abortion. Since it is easy to mischaracterize groups with whom you disagree, I want to ensure I accurately portray their stance. Essentially, AHA members are abolitionists. Anything short of the complete eradication of abortion is considered unsatisfactory. To this end, I agree. Where we part ways is in the methods used to achieve such a goal. While the pro-life camp is typically accepting of incremental laws that whittle away at abortion little by little, AHA is diametrically opposed to such bills. The main reason for this is because they feel it is showing partiality toward some babies while showing acceptance and compromise toward others. A perfect example would be the "heartbeat bill" that multiple states either recently passed or are currently looking at. The pro-life movement is generally in favor of bills such as these because we are willing to accept baby steps. At no point are they deemed satisfactory, but they are accepted as first steps toward a more comprehensive goal. However, as stated, AHA believes them to be wicked bills that dehumanize and promote the murder of babies without detectable heartbeats. While being a noble cause, it is misguided at best and deadly at worst.

Before we go any further, I find it important to remind us all that God is sovereign in all He does. In His infinite wisdom, He has allowed abortion to be legal in our country. Regardless of what happens from here, He is over all things. That fact does not negate our responsibility to care for the little ones and to be a voice for the voiceless (Proverbs 31:8-10). After all, that is the entire position of the pro-life movement. Yet, AHA (and others in the abolitionist movement) will openly declare this to be a foolish and wicked approach. If one were to say the end goal is to save lives, they will openly deny such a charge. In fact, they openly criticize pro-lifers as being willing to save lives at all costs. By "all costs," they mean being willing to accept incremental bills. While we declare incremental bills to be more palatable and more likely to be passed (which, in turn, saves some lives in the process), they believe, by promoting these bills, we are accepting evil and promoting the deaths of other babies so long as we save some. They claim these bills all take the approach of, "and then you have permission to kill your child." With this outlook, it is not hard to see why they believe us to be wrong. It sounds monstrous! But it is a strawman. Allow me to explain.

Abortion is currently legal in our country. We do not have to pass any laws to legalize the murder of prenatal babies, as it already exists. If a law is passed that prohibits the murder of prenatal babies of whom a heartbeat is detected, while allowing the murder of those of whom there is no heartbeat detected, it is not synonymous with creating a new law that legalizes their murder. Again, this is because that law is already on the books (whether one wants to acknowledge it as a valid law is irrelevant as the legal precedent has already been set). Passing such bills only means there now exists the potential to save countless babies in the first pass, and we are coming back to save the rest in the next pass (or however many passes it may take to achieve the end goal of abolition). It is whittling away at existing law and removing its power little by little when taking it head on would prove to be too much. A lumberjack does not go into the woods and demand an oak tree be felled. No, he swings his axe and, with each connection, removes a part of the tree. He continues to do this until the tree is too weak to stand and, finally, falls under its own weight. Just as an oak is brought down by incremental swings, so the path to abolition will be through incrementally removing the authority of existing abortion laws. By opposing such measures and tactics, abolitionists may be able to feel upright, just, self-righteous, and treating everyone equally, but all they really accomplish is equally leading all babies to the slaughter. This is not noble. It is illogical and wicked. It has more to do with the Pharisee in Luke 18:10-11 who, in his self-righteousness, was thankful that he was not "unjust" as the tax collector next to him. While maintaining a feeling of righteousness and pure justice, real human lives are being lost because they refuse to allow any law to pass that does not include all babies from being rescued in a single pass. Again, in their stubbornness, it only results in no babies being saved while they are afforded the opportunity to snub their nose in the air and mock those who are making every attempt to at least save one. Yes, if only even one is saved, it is all worth it as we continue making progress toward abolition. In all of my talks with abolitionists, the common theme is that they tend to live in an echo chamber of idealism while ignoring the reality of our society and laws.

In response to the argument made above, abolitionists have adopted the view that the U.S. Supreme Court does not make laws. This, they say, makes determinations such as *Roe v. Wade* a decision and not a law. Thus, if it is not a law, there is a no binding legislation that must uphold it. From there, the abolitionist will typically make claims that the states can individually decide whether or not to make abortion illegal. With this mindset, most abolitionists have taken their sight off overturning *Roe v. Wade*, and have since turned their attention to advocating for local law to pave the way to abolition.

In theory, this sounds like an appealing concept. After all, our Supreme Court has had nearly 50 years to overturn their 1973 ruling and, to date, have seemingly refused to do so. Unfortunately, it is just not true. In the United States, the Supreme Court is considered the final authority of interpretation of law. It is true that they do not create law, but they do have the final say when it comes to ruling on matters pertaining to the Constitution. As per U.S Constitution, Article VI, Clause 2, also known as the Supremacy Clause:

> This Constitution, and the Laws of the United States which shall be made in Pursuance thereof; and all Treaties made, or which shall be made, under the Authority of the United States, shall be the supreme Law of the Land; and the Judges in every State shall be bound thereby, any Thing in the Constitution or Laws of any state to the Contrary notwithstanding.[i]

Under the clause, the Constitution and the federal laws derived from it are considered the Law of the Land. While the Supreme Court does not make law, they do interpret the Constitution. With the way it was presented during *Roe v. Wade*, they interpreted it in favor of abortion under several Amendments. Thus, this became the definitive interpretation of the Law of the Land. Under the Supremacy Clause, judges in all states are bound by it. The only exception to this rule is if the Supreme Court determination is found to be unconstitutional. However, as we covered above, until the fetus is legally declared to be a person, the Supreme Court ruling is authorized to stand and all lower courts must submit to it.

Because of this, it makes little sense to appeal to the lower courts in an attempt to abolish abortion. The best that can be hoped for is a future set of Supreme Court Justices to reinterpret *Roe v. Wade*. Yet, even if it were to be overturned, this would not automatically make abortion illegal. All it would accomplish would be to remove the overarching declaration that states could not make it illegal. While the option would now exist to make it an illegal act, the State could also opt to keep it legal. I would be willing to bet my bottom dollar that states such as California and New York would continue down the same path they are currently on. I think the pro-choice community fears overturning the decision for two basic reasons. On the one hand, I truly believe many are ignorant. Just as abolitionists erroneously believe the states do not have to comply with the decision of the Supreme Court, some pro-choicers feel overturning it would automatically outlaw abortion. Sadly, this just is not the case. On the other hand, I believe there are those who understand this fact but enjoy having a buffer at the federal level. After all, why only have the State as a buffer when you can have a federal buffer as well? I feel those with this understanding fear a removal of one buffer would ultimately lead to a removal of the next. Realistically, even if *Roe v. Wade* is overturned, the pro-life community will still have plenty of work, as the only real solution is the personhood of the preborn.

With the overturning of *Roe v. Wade* looking highly unlikely, and such a definitive declaration of personhood even more so, we are presented with another option: incrementalism. Recognizing their inability to lawfully defy the Supreme Court interpretation, some states have opted to implement restrictions on abortion. These include parental consent, waiting periods, ultrasounds, heartbeat bills, partial birth abortion bans, trimester limitations, etc. While there may exist an inability to outright criminalize abortion-on-demand, that does not mean State legislators cannot implement policies meant to discourage it.

Because abolitionists believe the State does not need to follow the Supreme Court ruling, they will often argue any such policies are merely regulating abortion, thereby, allowing it. As I went over earlier, this just is not the case. It is already legal. No amount of restrictions can make it any more legal. They only serve to delay a legal process in hopes that some will change their minds. The pro-choice community is not blind to this fact. This is why they are continually trying to undo such restrictions. While abolitionists refuse to acknowledge the benefit of these restrictions, even a casual glace at the seething hatred of them by the pro-choice crowd should be enough to see the merit of having them in place. If they truly did nothing, and will lead to nothing, there would be no point in anybody being upset over them. But this is not a matter of restricting the movement of purple space elephants. This is a restriction of a very real process that has led to the death of millions. In the name of freedom, pro-choicers refuse to be impeded, and they know full well what might happen if abortion restrictions become accepted by the majority. As soon as culture accepts restrictions as beneficial, it becomes that much easier to jump to the next stepping stone. The agenda of the pro-choice community is to remove as many stepping stones as possible in an effort to ensure the stream can never be crossed. If they can see the threat of incrementalism, why is it that the abolitionist cannot?

Sadly, it appears the abolitionist movement is expanding into other groups and is no longer limited to the likes of AHA. While many of these new groups oppose the fanatical approach and tactics used by AHA (i.e. picketing churches), they have begun to adopt the view that incremental bills are wretched. In many of these groups, it is a blend of self-righteousness with the belief that incremental bills will not work and that we will lose precious time that could have been spent working on abolition bills. While I disagree on the likelihood of such "totality" bills passing, I can at least appreciate where they are coming from. Unfortunately, it still tends to be illogical and dangerous. For instance, one common objection to the heartbeat bill is that, since it is the abortion facility performing the heartbeat ultrasound, the technician will be more inclined to either skip the ultrasound altogether or purposely miss the heartbeat by performing the ultrasound in the wrong place. Essentially, the view is that the abortionist cannot be trusted. Therefore, the heartbeat bill is pointless and babies with a heartbeat will be aborted anyway. Is there any credibility to this argument? I dare say there is not. Let me explain why.

I can understand the skepticism which would lead one to assume the abortionist will purposely miss the heartbeat or perform the abortion anyway. It is a healthy sort of skepticism. However, it is also pure speculation rooted in their presuppositions. Think of it another way. People are always trying to find mechanic shops who are willing to fudge numbers to help a modified car pass a smog test. As much as mechanics are generally automotive enthusiasts and do not particularly like smog laws, finding a shop that will do it is extremely difficult. This is because most mechanics are not willing to risk losing their livelihood and being unable to put food on their table over a random customer.

Another example is gun shows. We have certainly all heard the "gun show loophole" but it is also a myth. I have personally bought a gun from a gun show and, even being active duty military at the time, I had to provide certain paperwork in order to get one. They were adamant that they could not sell me one without the paperwork being provided first to prove my residency in the city. Most licensed gun vendors are not willing to risk losing their license and affect putting food on their table all for a stranger. Will there be those who will do it anyway? Of course! However, they will be criminals and, if they get caught (be it by audit or by investigation after probable cause comes to light), they will face the consequences. I am very convinced most abortionists will play by the rules out of fear of losing their livelihood should they get caught. The statistics presented earlier should serve as enough evidence that laws and consequences do indeed inhibit the actions of the majority.

To add to this thought, if we are going to enter the realm of speculation, imagine how many pro-life pregnant women will receive a positive heartbeat ultrasound by a credible healthcare provider only to go to a mill and feign wanting an abortion in order to "catch" an abortionist telling her there is no heartbeat. They would be too easy to catch and prosecute. Again, most are not willing to lose their careers and negatively impact their family's way of life over a stranger. As it stands, most of the remaining abolitionist objections are rooted in the same flawed sense of logic.

As alluded to above, in addition to the belief that incremental bills will not work (contrary to what pro-choicers may think about them), many also hold the view that all laws must be righteous in nature. They argue that regulating abortion is unrighteous because it leaves some preborn to be left in their current circumstances, teetering on the edge of slaughter. While this is indeed a sad truth, the entire premise is built on faulty logic via an emotional appeal. If I see a car on fire, and there are multiple people inside, should I leave them all to burn if I determine I can only save one or two? What a horrendous thought!

Anybody worth their salt would clearly say it is better to save as many as we can than to save none at all. It is in this sense that I argue the abolitionist cares more about their flavor of righteousness than they do about saving actual lives. The sad irony is that the cost of this "righteousness" is the sacrifice of human flesh on the modern altar of Molech.

It is no coincidence that the most popular abolition organizations are also heavily composed of post-millennials. In a roundabout way, eschatology has found itself in direct ties with abortion. Most post-millennials I have encountered embrace varying degrees of theonomy. Literally meaning God's Law (*theos*: God, *nomos*: law), it sets forth the proposition that our civil magistrates must adhere to God's standard. This is to be accomplished through societal laws that reflect God's Law. Keeping this in mind, it is easy to see how the Christian might be inclined to follow it. For instance, Jeff Durbin (of Apologia Church and End Abortion Now) is a strong advocate for the system where he has affirmed his position that the only two options are theonomy or tyranny.[ii] With such well known Christians proclaiming the belief, does this give credence to it? I want to outright state I am certainly not advocating for antinomianism (i.e. lawlessness). I would be foolish to ignore the fact that God has written His moral law on the hearts of believers (Jeremiah 31:33; 2 Corinthians 3:3; Hebrews 10:16), and to a certain degree of conscience, unbelievers as well (Romans 1:32; 2:14-15). Specifically, as believers, we have an obligation to be obedient to the One who bought us with His blood (Galatians 3:13). However, what does that obedience look like and how far does it extend? Additionally, how much of the Old Testament Law should we be following today? If God truly reigns over all the earth (and He does), is theonomy a view that aligns with Scripture? I argue that it does not. I acknowledge theonomy comes in many flavors and varieties. For the purposes of this chapter, I am specifically referring to theonomic Christian Reconstructionism, which calls for implementing Mosaic civil penal code to our modern societal system. If you find yourself leaning toward theonomy, please read ahead with my stated intent in mind.

Personally, I think this form of theonomy becomes a dangerous position when taken to its fullest extent because it becomes inconsistent, mandates a theocracy, merges Church and State, and reintroduces what Christ has abrogated. I think it is a wonderful and necessary thing in the Church, but it has no place in the government as a formal requirement or system. If enacting a theocracy, it necessitates the reinstatement of civil Mosaic Law or else it is no longer grounded in biblical principles. After all, if we are going to mandate civil government follow the biblical structure as found in the Old Testament theocratic systems, we must also resurrect the biblical pattern for judicial consequences. Any other structure results in "cherry picking" and fails the test of consistency. However, our nation follows a system of separation of church and state, which means a theocracy can never be, as that makes the two a joint union.

Aside from feeling theonomy within government cannot be done properly, we have also never seen a single instance of it actually work, even in all of Scripture. Ultimately, sin gets in the way and leads to a perversion of God's Law, oftentimes leading to legalism, which is just as bad as antinomianism. It is impossible for us to live in a pure society that is fully governed by God. The only time we will ever see a functioning theonomy is in Heaven, and the only way to truly be a consistent theonomist is to conflate the Old Covenant with the New Covenant. While it may be understandable for a Presbyterian to start with such a premise (based to their belief that both the Old Testament and New Testament are the covenant of grace, just under two different forms of administration), the rising tide of Reformed Baptist theonomists is a bit of a mystery, as we see the two covenants as being distinctly separate with only the new being the covenant of grace. As Christians, we adhere to God's moral law as found in the Ten Commandments. While binding on all of creation, those not in Christ are expected to live like the world, and the day will come when they shall reap the judgment of their disobedience. While the moral law stands, the civil (and ceremonial) law has since been abrogated and, I argue, to adhere to theonomy is to minimize the completed work of

56

Christ. Furthermore, a theocratic government, if implementing theonomy to its fullest extent, would have to punish people for not being Christian, having a different sexual preference, etc. God will indeed judge spiritual rebellion and sexual immorality/homosexuality in His time, but our government should not assume that role. As Jeff Johnson has said, "Laws on stone do not change hearts of stone."[iii]

Every such form of implementation has failed, and there is a good reason for it. Let's break down a number of examples. At Creation, we see Adam and Eve before the Lord. They were in direct communion with Him and He was over them. He gave the command and their responsibility was to obey. That is a prime example of a theocracy how it was meant to be. However, we both know Adam and Eve failed miserably and paid the price that, ultimately, spread to all men in the form of physical and spiritual death. This wasn't a failure on part of the theocracy but of humanity. Yet, it still failed.

Throughout Scripture, we see more examples. For instance, the Hebrews followed Moses and submitted to the governing structure that was in place. This was another theocracy, as it was leadership appointed by God to lead His people. All moral, ceremonial, and judicial matters were handled by this body. While it was in effect for a time, Scripture reveals that Christ abrogated the ceremonial and civil law, leaving only the moral law that is written on the hearts of His own. Thus, we should not desire to go back to that construct as it is no longer functional.

While we see times of prosperity when the Old Testament kings of Israel feared the Lord and used discernment, we also see how they abused the position. Countless forms of sin crept in due to a sinful nature. This was a horribly perverted form of a theocracy that even God Himself warned against. Surely, this should not be advocated for if even God is against it (1 Samuel 8:7).

Now, let's skip ahead to the time of Christ and the early Church. While we see examples telling us to submit to the governing rulers because they were placed there by God, nowhere do we see a requirement that they be Christian in order to be legitimate. In fact, we even see evil rulers being regarded as legitimate. While they were indeed placed there by God, in no way was it a theocracy. Nor do we see Christ trying to implement a theocracy. What we do see is Christ setting the foundation for His Church and other New Testament passages telling us how we are citizens of Heaven (Ephesians 2:19; Philippians 3:20). If a theocracy was the structure in view here, Christ took zero time to speak of it and actually seemingly spoke contrary to it.

With that said, it has been argued that Jesus was a theonomist, and that He advocated for the system in Matthew 5:17. Does this undo everything I have just said and annul anything I am about to say, or are we just not thinking critically enough yet? First, think about the time period in which Jesus lived. The threefold division of the Law was still in effect. He was still performing His active obedience to the Law. With this in mind, we would be remiss to ignore the preceding verse where He says He, "did not come to abolish but to fulfill." Again, we cannot "cherry pick" the parts we want just to validate a belief. Keeping in line with the extent of Christ's vicarious atonement also comes the extent to which, as our federal head, His active obedience fulfilled the civil and ceremonial law. This becomes explicitly clear in Ephesians 2:15 when Scripture declares that Christ abolished the Law "composed of commandments expressed in ordinances." These ordinances were the decrees written in the handwriting of man (Colossians 2:14). This is a crucial detail that must not be overlooked. While man wrote the civil and ceremonial law, God Himself etched His moral law into stone. While there is still room for interpretation of *which* laws have been abolished, an all-or-nothing approach just does not work.

It must also be kept in mind that the civil law was only given to ethnic Israel for the purpose of preserving a people for the coming Messiah. Even before the Law was given to mankind, God's moral law still existed and sin was still in the world (Romans 5:13). This is because it is universal law that applies to all of humanity. Unlike the moral law, the civil law was only given to a specific people for a specific purpose. Not once do we see the early Church calling believers to uphold the Mosaic civil law. It is a concept that is foreign to Scripture. This is because they were not bound to it. Conversely, we do see Jesus making proclamation that the entirety of the Law rests on God's moral law (Matthew 22:37-39) is the foundation of all binding law.

While civil law has been fulfilled in Christ, this is not to say it has no virtue to it. As I said, I am not promoting antinomianism. Even the 1689 London Baptist Confession of Faith recognizes the civil law has a certain moral use to it through its general equity.[iv] But this does not mean believers are bound to observe it. This is because Christ fulfilled it in His active obedience. Believers are grafted into Him and His fulfilling of the civil and ceremonial law. There is only one aspect of the Law that we are now bound to: moral law.

Where we once again see a theocracy try to rear its ugly head is in the history of the Catholic Church. Within the first few centuries after Christ's death, the Church was the State and it handled all matters of governing ordinance. It was a true theocracy in every sense of the word. However, it, too, failed miserably due to human nature. It quickly became corrupt, lost sight of God, and sought absolute power, all while claiming the name of Christ. Perhaps even more frightening than the prospect of religion ruling over the people of the State is the thought of the State ruling over the people of the Church. Think it cannot happen? I highly suggest reviewing the history of Theodosius, c.391 A.D. When one conflates Church and State, man's sinful nature knows no bounds.

Yet again, it was an example of why a theocracy will never work this side of Heaven. The only example of a pure theocracy was in the Garden with God as the direct ruler and even that failed on the part of man. Every other instance was nothing more than a perversion of the theocracy we will see in eternity. And, as I stated above, to implement one on this earth necessitates a restoration of Mosaic civil law in order to properly punish the wicked who violate God's moral law.

The greater question becomes one of whether we are to hold the unbeliever accountable for violating God's Law. Clearly, we have consequences and punishments in place for things such as murder, rape, theft, etc. But is it in place because they violate God's Law or is it in place because they violate the law of the land? I would argue it is the latter, because punishment for violating God's Law will come from God Himself on the Day of Judgment. We still submit to it because we know the rulers are only there by God's divine appointment, but just as Pharaoh met his demise at the hand of God, so, too, will our ungodly earthly rulers. Again, no instance of a theocracy is necessary nor is it prescribed. We live in a pagan land with pagan rulers. While I would prefer a Christian be in office in order to possibly implement laws that honor God, I also recognize they are not obligated to do this. Similarly, if we had a Christian in office, I would not want the law of the land to be conflated with the standard of the Church. This would only open the door to punishing people solely for not being Christian or for worshiping a false god. Our civil government is not to be conflated with the moral law written on the hearts of those in the Christ. So where do we draw the line between good laws and bad laws? Must laws be rooted in the moral law in order to be good, or can they be completely separate and pagan in nature? While I argue that societal law need not enforce every infraction of moral law, we must still recognize that good laws will, by necessity of goodness, flow from it. While an important discussion, to even scratch the surface would detract from the overall scope of this book. For clarity's sake, know that while I do hold that good laws will stem from moral law, I also hold that not all moral law requires punishment and accountability by the civil magistrate.

I hope you can see why, though a beautiful term from the etymological position, theonomy is incredibly dangerous when implemented with an earthly system of government. We have many freedoms in this great nation and I value all of them, even the ones that give people the legal right to worship idols. While sounding liberating, due to its very nature, when taken to its logical and consistent end, it will always result in bondage to man and threatening of liberty. God indeed reigns over the earth and His righteous judgment will one day be executed in the day He withholds His grace and mercy. That day belongs to Him alone and not to any civil magistrates. There will come a day when Christ shall return and we will finally see theonomy as God intended. However, unless Christ comes back before sundown, today is not that day. While I readily admit not all abolitionists are theonomists or post-millennials, I have found it to be a common enough trend that it was worthy of exploring the tie-ins that it has with the topic at hand. Understanding the eschatological worldview can give great insight into the thought process of many abolitionists. Ultimately, I agree with David VanDrunen when he says:

> "The Kingdom of God proclaimed by the Lord Jesus Christ is not built through politics, commerce, music, or sports. Redemption does not consist in restoring people to fulfill Adam's original task, but consists in the Lord Jesus Christ himself fulfilling Adam's original task once and for all, on our behalf. Thus redemption is not 'creation regained' but 're-creation gained.'"[v]

As I draw to a close, I want to be very clear that I do not bring up theonomy as an attempt to give a thorough refutation of the system. A portion of a single chapter could never accomplish such a feat. I only bring it up as a way to initiating thought and encouraging further research by the reader. If it feels like a high level glossing over, that is because that was the intent. I also wish to reaffirm the fact that total abolition should absolutely be the end goal regardless of one's eschatological belief. If an abolition bill were to go up today, I would be in full support of it. However, I would not stop there, rest on my laurels, and consider my job complete. What if it fails? What if it fails repeatedly? Do we continue to play the same song on repeat or do we strategize and make a more effective plan? To be honest, I wish the pro-choice camp, back in 1973, had the same mentality as AHA and other abolitionists today. If that were the case, they would have demanded medical professionals have the legal right to leave babies of botched abortions to die on a table simply because they are unwanted. The likelihood of such an extreme bill passing in 1973 would have been nonexistent. Unfortunately, the pro-choice movement was rooted in incrementalism. What began as a divide within the church over feminism[vi] then shifted into a right to privacy and doctor/patient confidentiality in cases of abortion.[vii] This then paved the way for late term and partial birth abortions.

Until just recently, the above "extreme bill" was actually a reality. Abortionists were legally authorized to withhold medical treatment from babies of failed abortions, as they were left to die on the table. Thankfully, an Executive Order rooted in incrementalism overturned this heinous act, and doctors are now required to provide medical attention.[viii] Whether this order changes at some point remains to be seen, but we can at least be thankful it exists in the present. This is what it is going to take. Abortion will not be outlawed by a mob mentality. As highly as I can praise those who faithfully, week after week, stand outside abortion clinics to plead with mothers to be mothers and for fathers to actually be men, this alone will not change the law. In order to accomplish this, we need pro-life legislators in office. No, I don't mean those who wear the badge while opposing every abolitionist bill that comes their way out of fear of what will happen to their careers should they support it. These people are pro-life in title only. I am referring to valid pro-life legislators who have the overwhelming desire to see the eradication of abortion. On the local level, we need to continue to be an influence to those around us and help them see the horrific nature of abortion. As the local worldview changes, so shall the local votes. As the local votes change, so shall the laws. It may begin with us but we cannot do it alone.

While admitting it is not ideal, and though our theological ideologies differ greatly, I stand with Frank Pavone, of Priests for Life, when he declared:

> "The very principle of personhood, in fact, prevents me from sitting back and not protecting the lives I am able to protect right now. It is not by conceding an exception to their personhood that I protect them, but precisely because I embrace their personhood...All the while we seek to change the circumstances so that the steps are not so incremental."[ix]

Imagine where we would be as a nation today if AHA existed in the 1800's as Abolish Human Slavery. Imagine hearing of them picketing churches who opposed slavery merely because they felt the churches weren't doing enough to stop it. Imagine them openly condemning bills that sought the abolition of slavery through incremental means. If that had been the prevailing thought, slavery might still be legal today. Thankfully, the world had people like William Wilberforce who understood incremental bills were going to the path to final success. Admittedly, he eventually became opposed to them, but he did approve of them early on and saw their value. Even after he started growing more toward the abolitionist position and speaking out on incremental means, he still made concessions in areas that ended up demonstrably leading to a change of culture. Scott Mahurin, founder of Florida Preborn Rescue, summed it up nicely when he said:

> "Abolish Human Abortion essentially says either save all the babies or let them all die. Would William Lloyd Garrison or William Wilberforce advocate for this kind of fallacious "either-or" thinking? Either free every slave or free no slave? Would abolitionists during the antebellum era in America have resisted the Underground Railroad because it didn't save all the runaway slaves? Never. Would they have opposed legislation that outlawed slavery in some of the newly formed United States, in order to get the slave states cornered and surrounded

by anti-slavery states? No. They used pragmatic steps to achieve their ideological goals."[x]

Do not be fooled. It was the pro-choice movement's acceptance of incrementalism that led us to the horrific place we are at today. They knew it would work and they stood united in the cause. I say it is about time we steal their playbook and use incrementalism against them until they no longer have any power to stand. It may take a long time. Let's face it: our culture is not yet ready to end abortion. We should not have the expectation that the same culture that voted to legalize abortion would suddenly vote to outlaw it.[xi] We need to approach this topic with realistic expectations. That said, this fact should not stop us from standing united against abortion-on-demand, regardless how long it may take. Ronald Reagan once said, "Human life legislation ending this tragedy will someday pass the Congress, and you and I must never rest until it does."[xii] Though he fought for decades, Wilberforce died just before the abolition of slavery became a reality, but a reality it became.[xiii] If you are an abolitionist or a theonomist (or both), even if we disagree on that point, I hope you can at least find value in the rest of the book and the arguments within. Instead of fighting the pro-life crowd at the expense of human lives, stand united and take down the oak tree known as abortion, one swing at a time!

[i] United States Senate, *Constitution of the United States*, https://www.senate.gov/civics/constitution_item/constitution.htm

[ii] Apologia Studios, *Loving God's Law: Setting the Record Straight*, September 6, 2014, https://apologiastudios.com/apologia-radio/loving-gods-law-setting-the-record-E423WW6f

[iii] Jeffrey D. Johnson, *The Five Points of Amillennialism* [Conway: Free Grace Press, 2020], 98

[iv] The 1689 Baptist Confession of Faith, Chapter 19 - Of the Law of God, Paragraph 4

[v] David VanDrunen, *Living in God's Two Kingdoms* [Wheaton: Crossway, 2010], 26

[vi] R.C. Sproul, *Abortion: A Rational Look at an Emotional Issue* [NavPress, 1990], 152

[vii] Roe v. Wade, 410 U.S. 163, 1973

[viii] Sam Dorman, "Trump signs 'born alive' executive order aimed at protecting abortion survivors," *Fox News*, September 25, 2020, https://www.foxnews.com /politics/trump-born-alive-executive-order-abortion

[ix] Frank A. Pavone, *Abolishing Abortion: How You Can Play a Part in Ending the Greatest Evil of Our Day* [Nashville: Nelson Books, 2015], 160

[x] Scott J. Mahurin, *Bad Roots, Bad Fruits: A Pro-Life Challenge to AHA/Abolish Human Abortion* [Independently published: 2018], 82

[xi] Ibid.

[xii] Ronald Reagan, "Excerpts from President's Speech to National Association of Evangelicals," *New York Times*, March 9, 1983, https://www.nytimes.com/1983/ 03/09/us/excerpts-from-president-s-speech-to-national-association-of-evangelicals.html

[xiii] Paul F. Taylor, *A Pocket Guide to Social Issues: Wilberforce: A Leader for Biblical Equality* [Petersburg: Answers in Genesis, 2009], 69

Appendix A
Abortion: An Illogical and Unethical Conclusion

WHAT IS THIS?

The following is a college term paper I wrote in 2014. We were tasked with writing a commentary that utilized logic and rational thought supported by academic sources. Upon choosing my topic, the professor told me I had to choose another because abortion was a strictly emotional issue that could not be argued rationally. I challenged her to allow me to prove her wrong. Through much persuasion, she reluctantly agreed, informing me I ran a high risk of failing the class. My final grade, both for the paper and the class, was an A.

ABORTION: AN ILLOGICAL AND UNETHICAL CONCLUSION

Abortion. It's one of the few subjects that stir up controversy just by name alone. Rarely does a discussion on the matter end peacefully. Emotions run high and, before long, the discussion morphs into a debate which devolves into a heated argument. While unfortunate, it's to be expected on some level. In fact, many refuse to entertain such discussions in an attempt to avoid the inevitable argument. Is this a reasonable solution? Should we just ignore the cases being presented and pretend nothing is wrong? Do we agree to disagree and let bygones be bygones? Is there really a way to settle a debate that has been going on for decades?

Before one can truly form an educated opinion on the topic, I believe a proper understanding of the history and background is essential. Regardless of personal belief or conviction, where there is a lack of understanding, foolishness is almost certain to ensue. This is the birthplace of ill-informed decisions and misconstrued opinions based on faulty knowledge. Out of respect for the issue, I would like to take a few moments to review some of the history. Though I wish we could journey through the intricacies of the past together, due to space restrictions, we'll have to settle for a brief yet intriguing summary.

To begin, we first need to travel back in time to March 1970. There, we will meet a young woman who appears to be a relatively normal person upon first glace. Nothing seems to be out of the ordinary. However, what we don't know is that she is a single pregnant woman who is seeking to terminate her pregnancy in a state that has strict abortion laws. This "ordinary" woman, Norma McCorvey, is about to be known across the nation as Jane Roe (Rose, 2008, p. 93).

Roe had just filed a lawsuit against the District Attorney of Dallas County, Texas "on behalf of herself and all other women" claiming that her right to privacy was violated when held against the First, Fourth, Fifth, Ninth, and Fourteenth Amendments of the Constitution (Rose, 2008, p. 93) and that the existing abortion laws were preventing women from receiving adequate medical advice (Hitchcock, 2007, p.49). After an arduous three year battle, on January 22, 1973 (Davis, 2004, p. 141), the court ruled that, "For the stage prior to approximately the end of the first trimester, the abortion decision and its effectuation must be left to the medical judgment of the pregnant woman's attending physician." and "For the stage subsequent to approximately the end of the first trimester, the State, in promoting its interest in the health of the mother, may, if it chooses, regulate the abortion procedure in ways that are reasonably related to maternal health." (Roe v. Wade, 410 U.S. 163, 1973). Thus, abortion was now a private matter between the physician and the patient. Unless the patient was beyond the first trimester, there was little to nothing the state could do about it. Though the decision to terminate pregnancy ultimately rested within the hands of the physician, the power to choose was, for all intents and purposes, placed within the hands of the mother. Indeed, the future was about the change and, depending on your stance on abortion, it was either for the better or the worse.

So, here we stand today. It's been forty-one years since the court's decision and women have been free to obtain abortion-on-demand ever since. Likewise, the abortion debate has been waging equally as long, if not longer. As with all controversial topics, over the years, each opposing side has rallied with their peers to make their points, defend their positions, and stand their ground. In the beginning, I asked if this was a debate that could ever be solved. I dare say there is a plethora of ways to make the case that abortion is simply an illogical and inconsistent practice for anyone of sound mind. All we have to do is have the courage to peel back the curtain.

The reason it's such a heated topic isn't because of the nature of those discussing it. It's because of the nature of the discussion itself. It's more than trying to agree on fashion or debating which cereal tastes the best. Indeed, far more is at stake in this debate. We're dealing with human life. Whether or not one wants to admit it, regardless of the outcome, the very basis of the discussion is the topic of human life and all that goes with it. Even further, it is a discussion on the sanctity of human life. The focus may drift from time to time but, in the end, it always comes back to this point. While I admit this may be a bold assertion, I also truly believe objective logic and reasoning will show it to be both the central and essential point of the debate. Interestingly enough, of all the "friendly" discussions I've had over the years, the topic of doctor/patient confidentiality has yet to come up. It seems privacy was just the force required to get the snowball rolling downhill. For the sake of moving forward, I feel it's high time we review some of the arguments put forth by the pro-choice movement.

One common argument is that our country is already filled with neglected children and that we, as responsible adults, shouldn't be contributing to the problem. Part of the support for this stance is the claim that children born of unwanted pregnancies are prone to social and interpersonal difficulties (Faúndes & Barzelatto, 2006, p. 39). This is just absurd when you really think about it. What do acceptance and ease have to do with life? Should we now be authorized to execute those whom we deem undesirable? Many have said it isn't fair for a child to be brought into the world only to be rejected. Life isn't fair but that doesn't mean it ceases to be life. It is indeed a sad scenario when there is a young child who is neglected. We see countless stories of small children being taken away from their parents due to deplorable living conditions. Many of them even have disorders from years of psychological scarring. If one were to suggest we execute each one of these children as they're discovered, he would be viewed as an even worse monster than the deadbeat parents. Why, then, do we see this as such an honorable option? How can one possibly suggest it's nobler to destroy an unborn infant in an effort to prevent him from being born into an atrocious situation than it is to destroy a five-year-old who has been suffering in it for years? Why not end the misery of one and prevent the misery of the other? Where do we draw the line? Can it even be drawn clearly and distinctly? Of course, this may be a moot point if you aren't of the persuasion that the fetus is a human life. Thankfully, this will be addressed shortly so I ask you to patiently read on.

Second, many have taken the stance that abortion is an adequate, though controversial, solution to overpopulation in our society (McKinney & Schoch, 1998, p. 133). Some have even gone so far as to take this approach and claim, much like hunting is the answer to overpopulation of a given species in the wilderness, abortion is the answer to overpopulation in society. Are we now comparing ourselves to animal control? Are we once again choosing who needs to go? Are we now playing judge, jury, and executioner based solely off our own personal and private desires? The opinion of mankind changes with every breeze. Some may say gang wars should be a legal form of murder so long as no innocent bystanders get injured. Is it possible others may feel we should allow people older than a certain cutoff age to be murdered? After all, they've lived their prime and are of limited usefulness in most cases so far as a productive standpoint is concerned. Of course, I don't actually believe either of these and am only using them to make the point that killing other human beings isn't the answer. That being said, I've heard some claim support of the latter option and that, in my personal opinion, is no better than the pro-choice camp as both are suggesting a certain group is less deserving of life than another particular group of people. Even Margaret Sanger, who was instrumental in the founding of Planned Parenthood of America, believed birth control, a term she coined, was instrumental in controlling the birth rate of those whom she deemed inferior (Axelrod, 1999, p. 128). Is this where we stand today?

Third, and perhaps one of the most common arguments, we've undoubtedly all heard the claim that a woman has the right to do as she pleases with her own body. While this sounds like a very solid point, it's full of many holes. First and foremost, it isn't her body we're discussing. It's the body of the child inside her womb. Nobody is trying to tell her how she is to cut her hair. Nobody is trying to tell her she can't get a tattoo, sleep with as many partners as she pleases, or reserve herself for only one person. No, all of these are her rights and nobody can strip her of them. The pro-life camp isn't oppressing her in any of these ways. She isn't limited in the slightest when it comes to her rights. Yet, despite all this, she continually claims she is being oppressed. I suppose this all depends on how one defines oppression. If you define it as someone limiting your free actions in any way whatsoever, I would agree in full. Police officers are oppressing her. Lawmakers are oppressing her. In this case, any removal of choice without consequence would be defined as oppression. However, most would agree this is a necessary oppression to prevent us, as a society, from slipping into chaos and anarchy. Because of this differentiation, we must limit the definition of oppression to simply the limiting of one's rights. Does one have the right to take the life of another? Countless court verdicts shout a resounding no. How can a woman possibly imply her rights are being violated if the only limitation is her ability to destroy the unborn child within her womb? This is not a violation of rights. This is not oppression. If anything, each person is guaranteed the right to life, liberty, and the pursuit of happiness in the Declaration of Independence (US 1776). A similar assertion can be found in the Bill of Rights (U.S. Const. amend. V). Notice the key word: life. Before continuing, it's only fair to point out that developing fetuses are not currently protected under the aforementioned constitutional amendment simply because they are not deemed to be people until the point of viability. This is the direct result of the Supreme Court decision in *Roe v. Wade* (Sproul, 2010, p. 41). However, while the court may have ruled that the fetus isn't protected, does this ruling mean it shouldn't be? Rights are imbued to us all as human beings regardless of our age. As for the right to life, there is zero justification for taking it away without due process in a court of law. Since the infant has committed no crime, any charges against it should be instantly dismissed. There simply is no case. In the end, it isn't about a woman's ability to do as she pleases with her own body. It's about a woman's inability to do as she pleases to the body of another. Once she becomes pregnant, it's no longer about her body. This is just one of many red herrings meant to draw the attention away from the actual issue. Though, under our current laws, she may have the right to an abortion, we must always ask ourselves if simply having a right is synonymous with doing what is right. Furthermore, do we have the moral right to do that which is morally wrong (Sproul, 2010, p. 115)?

Fourth, there are those who simply do not believe the fetus to be a human life. Does this undo the pro-life stance? Is there any ground to stand on if the opposing side simply doesn't believe the same? After all, we can't force religion upon anybody. Is an atheist wrong if he doesn't believe in God and, as a result, chooses to not implement certain practices into his life? This appears to be the case many within this mindset are making. Thankfully, it is just another hollow argument. The evidence is mounted against them as are their inconsistencies. I've heard the fetus compared to cancer. They say it's nothing more than a clump of cells that are replicating into a mass. Since we have no problem removing these living cells during chemotherapy or surgery, it shouldn't matter if one chooses to have an abortion early on while the cells are still developing and replicating. It doesn't take much more than a glance to see the flaw in this logic. Cancer, while indeed growing, will always remain cancer. A surgeon will never remove cancerous cells only to find them crying on the surgical table and desiring to be comforted. Those particular cells, while being from a human, will never become a human. The same cannot be said of a fetus. By two weeks, the fetus has a discernable heartbeat. It has a unique blood type that is separate from the mother's. By six weeks the child has fingers at the end of each delicate hand, brain waves pulsing through a mind that is full of potential, and movement within the womb. By nine weeks, gender can be distinguished, a unique set of fingerprints have been created, and the baby has a fully functioning set of kidneys (Bosgra, 1987, p. 7-8). A heartbeat and brainwaves alone demonstrate life within an adult. Why is there such hesitation to apply the same determination to a developing embryo? Would this not simply be prenatal life (Sproul, 2010, p. 55)? Every last adult on earth began as this cluster of replicating cells and look at what we've become! From this perspective, the fetus is only at another stage of development in its life. A fetus is not an infant. An infant is not a toddler. A toddler is not a teenager. A teenager is not a middle-aged adult. A middle-aged adult is not a senior citizen. However, just because a toddler is not a senior citizen does not mean the toddler is not a human life. The same can be said of the fetus. It's a human being that is simply at an earlier stage of development in the life cycle. Despite this, many will say this isn't enough to prove anything. This has only opened the door for early term abortions vs. late term abortions using terms such as "point of viability" to justify it. Because of this, we must resort to logic and consistency. While I may not be able to prove beyond all shadow of a doubt, though all signs point to the affirmative, that the fetus is a human life, the pro-choice crowd is also unable to prove otherwise. Therefore, it boils down to responsibility. At the risk of overusing an analogy, I would like us to once again refer to the hunters mentioned earlier. Imagine two hunters in the woods that are hunting for deer. Hunter A sees movement behind a shrub but isn't certain what's behind it. He's fairly certain it's a deer and the law states that he's able to shoot it. Hunter B says he thinks it's another hunter but he can't be sure either. It moves like a person and seems to be exhibiting human tendencies but, due to limited vision, neither one is absolutely certain. Now, imagine Hunter A says he doesn't agree with Hunter B and wants to take the shot. Hunter B says he's fairly certain it's another person and that Hunter A shouldn't do it. Does Hunter A have the right to take the shot? Absolutely! However, it may not be without severe consequences. If it does turn out to be a human, he is now facing murder charges as well as recklessness with a deadly weapon. Ignorance won't be enough to overturn the guilty sentence. Furthermore, he wouldn't even be able to claim ignorance as he was warned numerous times by Hunter B. Sure, there is always a chance the "Hunter B's" of the world could be wrong but is the gamble really worth it when it comes to human life? Would you be willing to take the shot if you weren't absolutely certain whether or not it was a person you were taking out? Basic human responsibility should answer that one.

Finally, we can lay aside all the arguments and take a look at the emotional inconsistencies. There tend to be several categories of emotions. There are those who don't believe it to be human life and don't even feel the slightest tinge of guilt or remorse when they have an abortion performed. On the other side of the spectrum, there are those who do believe it to be human life and they feel extreme guilt and remorse post-abortion. These, I am convinced, are the only two consistent categories. The inconsistent categories would be those who do not believe it to be human life yet deliberate based on emotion as well as those who do believe it to be human life yet feel nothing. With the latter, this is simply no different than any other murderers out there as their own consciences have been seared. They fully believe the fetus to be life yet have justified the removal of life (killing) for reasons unknown. In the end, there is no justification for such a person as he would openly admit to "legal" murder. As for the former group, why do they feel emotionally torn if it isn't a human life? If they truly believe the fetus is just a clump of cells, there should be no remorse. There should be no deliberation. It should be a decision as simple as taking out the trash or mowing the lawn. Deciding whether or not to discard your beloved pair of pants should be more painstaking than whether or not to have an abortion. After all, you spent time breaking those pants in just right and you've had them for years. The fetus just got into your body recently. Either get rid of it and move on or decide to keep it, water it, and see what it grows into. Your emotions should only enter the picture after the baby is born for, prior to this, it's not a life so there is no reason to be emotionally attached. To be honest, this emotional turmoil in the life of one who is pondering an abortion is a sign that she truly does believe the fetus to be a human life regardless what she may claim when asked in public. Her conscience has already betrayed her. At this point, we once again enter the realm of moral and ethical responsibility as made in the previous point.

So, where do we go from here? Do we continue to stand by idly as we hear of neglected children having no place in this world? Do we declare open season on those we deem inferior? Do we continue to allow the right to privacy to trample a child's basic right to life? Is it time to hold people accountable for their irresponsible and reckless actions? Sadly, these are questions each of you must answer for yourself. As I stated in the beginning, abortion is a highly emotional topic. Perhaps you've gone through with an abortion of your own. If you felt no remorse, my hope is this commentary has given you something to chew on. However, if you felt even the smallest tinge of guilt, my hope is that you will be convinced, now more than ever, that a fetus is an intricately crafted human being that is fighting against all odds for survival. Let us be a voice for the voiceless and stand against abortion. Any other option just doesn't make sense.

Appendix B
Real Talk

WHAT IS THIS?

The following is a collection of real-life discussions I have had with others on the topic of abortion. These transcripts are meant to demonstrate what you might encounter should you decide to take what you have learned and apply it to dialogue with those who oppose the pro-life position. Think of the beginning of this book as equipping you with the tools necessary to become involved in the dialogue. This next part is just meant to give a taste of how you might apply it. It consists of thirteen examples. Each example begins with an opening statement and the context, followed by how that particular discussion played out. For the most part, the discussions are shown as they were typed, only censoring foul language and correcting spelling/grammar for readability.

Example #1

OPENING STATEMENT:

Travis Rogers: If you applaud and support this, you have immeasurable evil in your heart. PERIOD.

CONTEXT:

Article with headline stating, "Lawmakers pass bill to protect abortion rights in NY."[i] The bill removed every instance of the term "abortion" in their penal code while also disqualifying it from being a valid court case. Thus, it explicitly allows abortion up until 20 weeks while also explicitly removing the illegal nature of having one performed after 20 weeks which now implicitly allows late-term abortions under law.

DISCUSSIONS:

Phillip: "immeasurable evil". That's a pretty bold claim.

Travis Rogers: Bold indeed and I stand by it. Feel free to dispute it and I'll gladly discuss it but just know that I stand by my statement.

Phillip: First, I need to know specifically why you believe someone supporting this has evil in their heart.

Travis Rogers: Because a matter of 5-6 inches and a span of 30 seconds doesn't magically turn "not life" into life. Therefore, to support the killing of a fully developed baby that can survive on its own (or with the help of the NICU), all in the name of freedom, is vile to no end and necessitates one having evil in their hearts. No right person would ever wish such evil on another, let alone a child. You've already told me you don't support late term abortions. Now is your time to ask yourself why you feel that way. A pregnant woman at 40 weeks set to deliver tomorrow can now kill her child this evening and face no legal repercussions. It's sick!

Phillip: *"Because a matter of 5-6 inches and a span of 30 seconds doesn't magically turn 'not life' into life."*

You'll need to elaborate on that a little more.

Travis Rogers: Meaning the distance of the birth canal and how short delivery can be in some cases.

Phillip: But then you could make the argument of "a sperm entering a uterus doesn't magically turn 'not life' into life."

Travis Rogers: Except that's exactly how it works. That's the very science behind it. *Phillip*, don't stand up for murderers. You've already told me you reject late term abortions. This time, your party has gone too far.

Phillip: We can have that discussion elsewhere. In this thread, I particularly want to know the thinking behind your statement that someone like me has "immeasurable evil" in my heart. Give me your take on that.

Travis Rogers: Because it takes immeasurable evil to justify this law and. If one can justify this, there's no limit to what they will support if their ilk pursue and press the idea long enough. My challenge to you is to list one shred of evidence that says a 40 week gestational fetus isn't a human life. I could list many on the contrary but this is a challenge for you. It simply can't be done without really reaching for an answer. It's not a belief that the baby isn't real but immeasurable evil in their hearts that justifies the action in the name of freedom.

Phillip: That challenge is irrelevant to me as I don't believe at 10-months the baby is not a viable human being. As far as I can tell, this law they passed protects late-term abortions in special emergency cases, not just at-will.

Travis Rogers: Have you read the bill along with all the all the amendments? It's true the following statement is there:

- "the patient is within twenty-four weeks from the commencement of pregnancy, or there is an absence of fetal viability, or the abortion is necessary to protect the patient's life or health."

However, the bill also:

- Removes the term "abortion" from the heading that used to read HOMICIDE, ABORTION AND OTHER OFFENSES.

- Removes the phrase "or an unborn child with which a female has been pregnant for more than twenty-four weeks" from the definition of homicide in reference to someone's conduct causing the death of the above.

- Removed "abortion in the first degree or self-abortion in the first degree" from the definition of homicide.

- Removed all traces of the term "abortion" from the penal code.

- Removed the term "abortion" from court sitting procedures signifying it's no longer an issue for the court.

When *Roe v. Wade* occurred, it was under the pretense of doctor/patient confidentiality. It was nothing more than the push for the snowball. After all, of all the arguments from the pro-choice crowd, how often do you see their major push being privacy with their doctor? I've yet to see that be the main argument. That's because it was never the main intention. The same goes for the first statement. Yes, it says twenty-four weeks but their systematic removal of words and phrases has effectively made it legal up until birth since it's no longer unlawful in any degree.

Put it this way: Speeding is illegal but certain speeds will net you reckless driving. If a law goes into effect that says you can speed up until 20 mph over the limit but that all reference to speeding has also been removed from the law books, that now means you can drive at any speed you want without repercussion. They did the same thing

83

with abortion. They said it's legal up until 24 weeks while, simultaneously, striking any law prohibiting it from occurring at any point thereafter.

Phillip: Yeah, that's pretty much the point. You want people that perform or have any abortion at any point during pregnancy to be punished under the law (to whatever degree you think that should be). Your views go in the opposite direction and any small "push" would be a win in your book if it pushed towards criminalizing all abortions. Your views being elementary as they ignore grown humans and protect potential "humans" (not getting into definitions right now as it seems arbitrary at the moment). Cut and dry, you want criminalization of abortions. No compromising, no philosophical admissions in any direction.

So, bringing this back to me being immeasurably evil. I honestly want to know if you really believe me to be immeasurably evil. I support abortions in certain circumstances. My views take in whatever information I can in order to make a good moral decision on the issue. Right now, the science seems unclear on the issue of the viability of a being inside the matrix of a women at certain points during the pregnancy. Since this is the case, I have to make a judgement on this information towards a morally just decision. My intentions are safety, less harm and less dying. If abortions turn out to be murder, then I will not support abortions and will side with you on the concept of criminalizing abortions.

Travis Rogers: Man, get real here. We may disagree but, since we're friends, I'm going to call you out. Your very own post right there was filled with more holes than Swiss cheese. You said, "I support abortions in certain circumstances." Yet, you support this bill that says it's okay in all circumstances. Therefore, if you support this bill, you support ALL circumstances with zero limitations or hesitation. Don't try telling me you only support it in certain circumstances unless you're ready to stand against this bill.

You said, "The science seems unclear." I'd be curious what science you're referring to because literally every shred of evidence points toward the fetus being a life, at a minimum, by the point of viability. We can argue any time period prior to that ever-shifting point but there's zero argument after it in any credible scientific or medical position.

You said, "My intentions are safety." If that were true, you'd be highly concerned with knowing with absolute certainty that you weren't advocating the death of a child. Your cavalier attitude tells me you don't care about safety nor do you care about finding out whether the fetus is life. And, if you do, your inconsistency is showing. If you really cared about less dying, you'd be doing everything you could to be certain that our laws accurately reflect reality when it means a life is potentially on the line.

By this current law, a physician can abort a breech baby with its feet sticking out so long as it isn't fully born and there's nothing in the penal code to prevent that from happening. If you don't find that to be a reprehensible evil, yes, you would have to have immeasurable evil in your heart. I pray that isn't the case and that you're just too afraid to dare cross your party line or call out the evil from within. We recently had this conversation and you rejected such an idea as being immoral. Yet, here we are and you're now backpedaling to fall in line with the mob.

Phillip: Wait, what? You just admitted before that, that the bill has conditions.

"the patient is within twenty-four weeks from the commencement of pregnancy, or there is an absence of fetal viability, or the abortion is necessary to protect the patient's life or health."

85

You said every shred of evidence points toward the fetus being a life, at a minimum, by the point of viability. Then send me the links. I didn't save any of the information I've looked at because it's been freelance and random. I haven't had much interest in the issue until recently where people like you started making claims about this.

You said, *"If that were true, you'd be highly concerned with knowing with absolute certainty that you weren't advocating the death of a child."* My god I think I've struck a nerve. Throwing passive-aggressive insults at me. I do that s*** too, so I know why it's done. I know for a fact that you know what the word "intentions" means. You are telling me that you know my intentions are not what I say they are because I don't know with absolute certainty that I am advocating the death of a child. I know you read my comment where I literally said "If abortions turn out to be murder, then I will not support abortions and will side with you on the concept of criminalizing abortions." But nah, I'm totally lying about my intentions. Having a civil discussion and all, or at least trying to, and being open about my lack of knowledge on the issue. Trying to pull out more information from you for my own personal education. But yeah, I'm sitting here lying about my "intentions."

This isn't supposed to be a butt-hurt discussion. If you have information that can change my mind, present it. You sent links before, but I lost them. I usually leave my computer on all night and the next day my girlfriend usually closes my tabs. Send links. Give information. Or sit there on a high horse of superiority and believe with all your heart that I have the blackest most evilestest heart and mind because I support some abortions. I'm not reading the rest of the comment. I just want links and information.

Travis Rogers: Maybe you missed the rest of my post (which you already admitted you didn't read). What you interpreted in the bill as limitations is actually just explicit permission. Meanwhile, there's implicit permission in any circumstance up until birth because they removed they rest of the law that once prevented it. Essentially, they're telling people they can do it up until 24 weeks while also telling people it's no longer against the law to do it after that either. Therefore, that statement is irrelevant and is meant to detract attention from what they were really passing which is guilt-free abortion for any reason at any point up until birth.

It makes me righteously angry that over 40,000,000 babies to date have been murdered and now our law is allowing it up until birth. However, my response to you wasn't made in anger as much as it was pointing out how inconsistent your claims are. At least you finally admitted to this not even being on your radar until recently. However, I find that hard to believe considering we've been having this discussion for years and you were even once pro-life and disgusted by the thought of abortion. That's because you knew the fetus was a human life and you were able to justify it and articulate it clearly. However, if that's the position you're going for, I'll go with it. If you want links, I'll send you things. My concern is that, if you're not even willing to read a single post, I'm not so sure you'll read any links I send.

Phillip: Yes, when I was against abortion, it wasn't based on science. I didn't know any of the science behind any of it. It seemed like to moral standing to take given my religious views. If you send links, I really will read them. However, I take my time with things because the links you send me are not the only thing I will be researching. What I normally do is look through whatever sources are touched on in the links themselves. After going through some of the material, if I have questions about a finding, I contact the person via email and ask them for elaboration or more data. It's not just a "read, read, read... whelp, that settles it!"

Travis Rogers: I still find it baffling how there are more indicators that the fetus is a human life than there are signs to the contrary yet, while you sit in peaceful and time consuming research, you advocate for abortion to remain legal to the point of birth instead of opposing it (at least to a certain degree) for the sake of potential children you're allowing to be slaughtered. You claim ignorance on the topic and the evidence shows people are dying in the process. Even if they were only potentially dying, I'd be erring on the side of caution. Sadly, in this case, not taking a position is the same as advocating for it.

---

[i] Associated Press, *Lawmakers pass bill to protect abortion rights in New York*, January 22, 2019, https://abc7ny.com/5101436/

Example #2

OPENING STATEMENT:

Travis Rogers: It's no coincidence that NY passed that law today of all days. While those with morals mourn the murdered children, the putrid celebrate the anniversary of *Roe v. Wade* by further legalizing their wretched ways of death. Am I angry? You bet!

CONTEXT:

New York passed new abortion legislation on the anniversary of *Roe v. Wade*.

DISCUSSIONS:

Matthew: "those with morals" Morals are subjective.

Travis Rogers: If morals are subjective, they don't exist at all. If they don't exist at all, there is no possibility for anyone to be wronged. If there's no possibility for anyone to be wronged, there's no need for laws. If any one of these are deemed necessary, it means absolute morality must exist.

Matthew: There's not even close to such a thing as absolute morality in this case.

Travis Rogers: You'll need to justify that statement because I obviously don't agree with it nor do I follow the logic.

Donald: *Matthew* I bet you don't live your life as if morals are subjective.

Matthew: *Donald* I live my life based on my personal morals. But are my morals the same as your morals or *Travis'* morals? Probably not since we disagree on this topic. Thus, there is no absolute morality here, otherwise we would agree on the abortion topic.

Donald: So, you would not make a moral judgement about Nazi Germany, Communist Russia, rape of Nanking, American slave trade, etc.? If someone hurt a loved one or stole your property, don't pretend like you would not want justice or restitution. You live inconsistent with your worldview.

Matthew: What does abortion have to do with those topics? I said there is no such thing as absolute morality with abortion. Prove me wrong, don't change the subject.

Donald: Abortion is the murder of a human life. Murder is absolutely wrong. Abortion is absolutely wrong.

Matthew: Incorrect.

Donald: Do you believe murder is immoral?

Matthew: Murder is wrong. But an abortion is not murder. Thus you are wrong.

Donald: If morals are subjective, then why is murder wrong?

Matthew: Changing the subject again? We're talking about abortion, not murder. Please stay on point.

Donald: You are denying that abortion is the intentional killing of a human life, despite all scientific evidence.

Matthew: So what you are saying is that my morals on abortion differ from yours. Thus, you have proven my point that abortion is not an absolute morality.

Donald: First you said morals are subjective. Then you said murder is wrong. Then you claim abortion, which is murder by its very definition, is not wrong. You are confused, bro.

Matthew: No confusion here. Abortion is murder by YOUR definition.

Donald: At least my worldview is a consistent one.

Matthew: *So* you think, but unfortunately you're not consistent with the rest of modern civilization.

Travis Rogers: *Matthew* I know you keep trying to stick solely within the topic of abortion but, by doing so, you're missing the greater point being made. Morality must always be absolute for, if it's subjective, it's no longer morality but personal preference. Thus, morality isn't dictated by laws, personal beliefs, personal preferences, or popular opinion. It either exists as an absolute in every area or it falls completely and doesn't exist whatsoever. If the latter, laws are now pointless as nobody can be found guilty of wronging. The option ceases to exist. This is the greater point being made. By saying there's no absolute morality on this subject, it necessitates you discarding morality completely in every subject.

If science and medicine consider a 40 week fetus to be a human life and the baby can survive on its own outside of the womb, on what ground do you stand to say the forceful removal of said life isn't murder? Maybe the better question is how do you constitute life? While the reality of the answer has no bearing in any of our personal beliefs, I'm curious what your answer is. What constitutes life?

Donald: *Matthew* Modern civilization is inconsistent with itself and suppressing the knowledge of its creator.

(There were no further responses from Matthew)

Example #3

OPENING STATEMENT:

A shared article stating:

"If you're mad about the new abortion law in New York please take a minute to read this. You're probably picturing the horrible women who decide last minute that they in fact don't want to be mothers and decide to kill their baby instead. I understand why that image makes you angry so please look at these ones instead.

After having 2 miscarriages, I almost died giving birth to my stillborn daughter. She had a genetic problem that was not compatible with life outside of the womb. We had no idea until she died at 32 weeks. Recovery was hard, I had an emergency c section and lost more than half my blood. We stayed in the hospital for a week, until my levels were okay enough to spend the next 6 weeks at home on bed rest, grieving my daughter.

I'm 15 weeks pregnant now and if we find out that this baby has the same genetic issues as our last then we will be faced with the difficult decision of terminating the pregnancy or again possibly almost dying giving birth to a stillborn baby.

So I just wanted to show you who this law is for. It only allows for late term abortions of babies that are going to die anyway or for pregnancies that might kill the mother.

This law is for the women who have been struggling for years to have a healthy baby, only to find out at the end of their pregnancy that their baby won't survive, or that if they continue the pregnancy they will probably die. This law will give women a little bit of control of something so horrible happening to them. This law will save lives of women like me."[i]

CONTEXT:

An article making a false claim about the purpose of New York's abortion bill.

DISCUSSIONS:

Travis Rogers: The article does a great job of tugging at heartstrings. Sadly, it destroys any credibility when it gives a patently false statement as its entire premise.

I read every word of the bill to include all edits for a before and after comparison. In regard to the statement your article made claiming the bill only impacts extreme emergencies, if you truly read the bill along with all the all the amendments, you will see the following. It's true that the following statement is there:

- "the patient is within twenty-four weeks from the commencement of pregnancy, or there is an absence of fetal viability, or the abortion is necessary to protect the patient's life or health."

However, the bill also:

- Removes the term "abortion" from the heading that used to read HOMICIDE, ABORTION AND OTHER OFFENSES.

- Removes the phrase "or an unborn child with which a female has been pregnant for more than twenty-four weeks" from the definition of homicide in reference to someone's conduct causing the death of the above.

- Removed "abortion in the first degree or self-abortion in the first degree" from the definition of homicide.

- Removed all traces of the term "abortion" from the penal code.

- Removed the term "abortion" from court sitting procedures signifying it's no longer an issue for the court.

When *Roe v. Wade* occurred, it was under the pretense of doctor/patient confidentiality. It was nothing more than the push for the snowball. After all, of all the arguments from the pro-choice crowd, how often do you see their major push being privacy with their doctor? I've yet to see that be the main argument. That's because it was never the main intention. The same goes for the first statement. Yes, it says twenty-four weeks but their systematic removal of words and phrases has effectively made it legal up until birth since it's no longer unlawful in any degree.

Put it this way: Speeding is illegal but certain speeds will net you reckless driving. If a law goes into effect that says you can speed up until 20 mph over the limit but that all reference to speeding has also been removed from the law books, that now means you can drive at any speed you want without repercussion. They did the same thing with abortion. They said it's legal up until 24 weeks while, simultaneously, striking any law prohibiting it from occurring at any point thereafter.

Randy: I read your post and conversation about the bill. While I agree it is tragic that they include way too many loopholes and avenues for abuse involving non-medical emergencies, I have known someone personally who had to make the decision of watching her infant suffer for the first few breaths before dying or aborting the baby before birth. Unfortunately, she doesn't get to choose what stage in pregnancy the medical condition was discovered. I agree the bill allows for abuse, but it does provide some lifesaving solutions for mothers.

Travis Rogers: The bill does more than allow for abuse. It was written for that purpose. I suspect it's in preparation for the (however unlikely) possibility of a *Roe v. Wade* overturn so they can point to their pre-existing state law. All that they purposefully removed speaks louder than the very small line they added. Ultimately, they sought to remove any penal consequences for abortion at any time for any reason.

As for your friend, it's never easy to see a child die. However, if my child gets sick and only has a week left to live, I shouldn't be authorized to have someone put him down before I get home from work to avoid me watching him die. Nor should I be authorized to kill him in his sleep that night to avoid him having to experience his own natural death at the end of the week.

As for life saving solutions for mothers, modern medicine and science has stated there is almost no case where the pregnancy will actually kill the mother. This is further underscored given modern medicine and treatment. In the EXTREMELY rare case that it's a guarantee that death to the mother will occur, I may concede some ground but the chances are so incredibly rare that it's almost unheard of among all pregnancies that occur every year. It's a talking point based in emotion that is meant to convey the idea that it's commonplace and, therefore, valid. However, the reality is that it's so incredibly rare that most examples are hypothetical. This alone hurts the credibility and validity of the argument. No rule should ever be based on an exception so rare that it requires hypotheticals in order to discuss it.

Kirstin: *Travis Rogers* I believe you should do some research on maternal mortality rates. The fact that you said it is extremely rare that a woman dies from pregnancy is not true. Every individual case is different of course and there are many factors that come into play, but it is not as rare as you think.

Travis Rogers: *Kirstin* Based on the numbers provided by the CDC, in 2009, the were around 6,369,000 pregnancies in the U.S. Based on your first reply, the number of annual maternal deaths (of which they state includes not just pregnancies but also complications that may arise post-partum when the baby is already alive and protected by law) comes to 700 per year. By the math, that means the grand collective of deaths is 0.01099073%. That's an incredibly small percentage to be using as if it's a mainstream argument and enough of an epidemic to justify murdering nearly 1,000,000 people per year.

Kirstin: Yes, and like I said every case is different. There are many complications when it comes to pregnancy, while the child is in the womb and postpartum. I work in healthcare and I'm also a woman. If I was pregnant and I was told my child would have a very high chance of not surviving after birth I would like to have the CHOICE to have my own right to decide what happens to my body and my child. Instead of being forced to carry on to term and thinking about how my child is going to suffer when I give birth. That is why the law was made. It is to help protect those types of situations. To help women have the right to their own bodies and choices.

Travis Rogers: Regardless if every instance is different, that still only equates to 0.01099073% of all cases. You said it's not as rare as I might think and that my statement isn't true. If I told you that you had a 0.01099073% chance of being into a car accident on your next drive, I imagine you'd say that was an incredibly rare chance that would be hardly worth taking into account when it came to your decision to drive or stay home that day. This is further amplified by the fact that in abortion a woman is saying she should raise the death toll of her baby to a 100% chance in order to avoid her 0.01099073% chance. The reality is that, even as low as the numbers are, the majority of all abortions aren't to avoid a 0.01099073% chance of risk but are merely a matter of convenience.

You stated you're a woman but that's already a flawed argument as it's a false appeal to authority, as if being a woman gives you more insight into whether or not the baby is truly alive. Yes, as a woman, you will have more hardship than a man but it doesn't make a baby any more or any less of a baby. Thus, it's a moot point in this discussion. You're free to do whatever you want with your body so long as it doesn't result in the death of another person. Hence, why I can't take my body and ram somebody off the road for cutting me off in traffic. I can change lanes all I want but I'm not free to change lanes into another car. Your choices, should you ever choose abortion, don't determine life. They merely violate it and, ultimately, forcefully remove it against the freedom and choice of the one you decide to kill.

Kirstin: Sometimes you are faced with hard decisions in life that are in fact life and death decisions. I deal with those types of decisions in the care of human beings every single day. I don't feel that the fact that I am a women presents a flawed argument. Yes, we have to deal with things differently than men do and that's something men will actually never understand. You will never be able to feel a child inside your body, as I have. You will not know the emotional turmoil of bonding with a child inside of you and it potentially dying in utero or after birth. Those are factors that you will not understand, in my opinion. I understand regardless it's a baby. But as a mother I am obligated to do what is best for MY child whether that be while in the womb or outside of it. And I don't feel like anyone else outside of myself and the man who helped me make a child should have any influence on the potential future of our child's life. At the end of the day our baby does not really truly matter to anyone else except the fact that they are a baby with a heartbeat. There are thousands of babies around the world dying every single day, but outside of our country it's basically out of sight out of mind.

Travis Rogers: So, the fundamental basis of your argument is, as the mother, being free to do what is best for your child. I'd be curious why you think "mercy killing" is truly what's best for the child. Sickness and disease is simply a sad fact of life. We don't go around killing all the diseased people as an act of mercy. I can't kill my teenage child as an act of mercy. Should she become terminally ill, the best thing I can do for my daughter is comfort her, love her, and cherish what little time I have to be with her. The thought of killing her for mercy would never enter my mind nor should it ever. Therefore, why would it make sense in this case?

Notice that we've now shifted away from the topic of maternal death and have slid into the topic of disease and fetal/infant mortality. That's how it works with this topic. Once the topic of fetal/infant mortality is proven to be non sequitur, it'll shift into another equally as baseless point. In the end, no amount of data or consistent logic will suffice because it all boils down to the woman not wanting to be told what to do. That's because abortion is the bitter fruit of feminism. There's really only one viable outcome and it's the illegalization of abortion.

---

[i] Destiny Young, *Facebook*, January 24, 2019,
https://www.facebook.com/destiny.boisvert/posts/2266342413387002

Example #4

OPENING STATEMENT:

Travis Rogers: Sad fact.

CONTEXT:

A photo of a billboard paid for by Planned Parenthood that states, "I had an abortion, and I am not apologizing." Somebody edited it to say, "I killed someone and I am not apologizing."

DISCUSSIONS:

Matthew: Who is this 'someone' she 'killed'? What is his or her name and social identity number? We need to get the police on this matter if she actually killed a full-fledged human!

Henry: *Matthew* The Unborn Victims of Violence Act of 2004 (Public Law 108-212) is a United States law which recognizes an embryo or fetus in utero as a legal victim, if they are injured or killed during the commission of any of over 60 listed federal crimes of violence. The law defines "child in utero" as "a member of the species Homo sapiens, at any stage of development, who is carried in the womb." What we have here is the answer to your question about the "full-fledged human." The argument here is about the definition of crime and enforcement of punishment...as abortion currently does not fit the crime regardless of the current legal "full-fledged" human status of a fetus. Feel free to ask more questions if you are still confused.

Matthew: That law recognizes an unborn child as a legal victim for the purpose of penalizing the offender. i.e.: prosecutors going after a man for murdering a woman and her unborn child for TWO counts of murder. The law does NOT apply towards abortion, since abortion is not one of the 60 listed federal crimes. Try again.

Henry: Why don't you try reading my comment again?

Travis Rogers: *Matthew* Read carefully what you just wrote. Essentially, it leads to you believing nobody has the right to kill a human being except his/her mother. Crime criteria doesn't determine humanity. Nature alone does that. The baby can't be both a human and not human at the same time depending on who is asking. Life doesn't work that way, ignorance does.

Matthew: It's important to understand how to read and understand the purpose and definition of laws. The law quoted above is to penalize those responsible for committing any of the 60 federal crimes listed within it against unborn children. For the sake of penalizing those who commit said crimes, the unborn children are considered a member of the human race. That does NOT mean that all unborn children are ALWAYS defined as such; only when THIS PARTICULAR LAW is utilized. Abortion is not one of the 60 listed federal crimes, thus yes, a mother does have the right to make a decision on ending her pregnancy, a decision which is supported by its own federal law.

Henry: *Matthew* If you read my comment you will see that it already acknowledges what you just said. If you read *Travis'* comment you'll see that he's talking about a moral right, not a legal one. I read your comment and I agree with you. It is important to understand how to read.

Matthew: That's because *Travis* wishes laws were based on religious scripture instead of democratic policy.

Travis Rogers: This is where critical thinking comes into play. Personally, I enjoy thinking through things instead of letting the government do it for me. That's not necessarily a knock on you personally as much as it is a statement. Even a cursory glance can see the inconsistency with the law's application. One isn't simultaneously both a human and not a human. The Law of Noncontradiction mandates this. Additionally, crimes committed against a person don't dictate their personhood. They only dictate the crimes committed.

Therefore, if a fetus is a human being, the argument stops being one of whether or not the law calls it such and more of whether or not the law needs to be better defined. I argue that a rock should never be treated as a human as it simply isn't. Similarly, if a fetus isn't a human, the law should NEVER state that it is. However, since it clearly does recognize the humanity of the fetus at times, we now must admit that, if it's correct in those moments, out of necessity, it dictates that it's incorrect in the moments when it does not. Either the fetus is ALWAYS a human and deserves the same protective rights as any other human or it's NEVER a human and should be treated as any other piece of property. Those are the only consistent options. Considering all science and medicine point to the fetus being a living human and there is already legal precedent of the fetus being treated as such, we should all be fighting for laws to change in order that innocent and defenseless humans are protected and that their basic human rights (in this case, the right to life) stop being violated, by their own mothers no less.

Travis Rogers: *Matthew*, where have I mentioned the bible or religion in this thread? That's a cop out and you know it.

Matthew: You don't have to mention it for it to be the source of your agenda.

Travis Rogers: It's absolutely the source of why I care about human life. However, it need not be stated to point out the absurdity of the contrary position in this debate.

Travis Rogers: Thought I'd leave this right here:

"HHS accomplishes its mission through programs and initiatives that cover a wide spectrum of activities, serving and protecting Americans at every stage of life, from conception."

SOURCE: U.S. Department of Health and Human Services

Mitchell: *Matthew* why not deal with the arguments *Travis* presented?

Travis Rogers: *Mitchell* Because casting a smokescreen tends to be the default for many when a logical presentation can't be refuted.

Example #5

OPENING STATEMENT:

Travis Rogers: Went with a friend to the local abortion mill to share the gospel and speak the truth in love regarding the human child they were preparing to slaughter. Sadly, we were met with much hatred and anger. The clinic volunteers scorned us and openly laughed/mocked us. Drivers flipped us the bird as they drove by. It was quite the experience. I suppose none of it should've surprised me.

John 15:18

If the world hates you, you know that it has hated Me before it hated you.

1 Corinthians 1:18a

For the word of the cross is foolishness to those who are perishing

CONTEXT:

An angry response to a visit to the local abortion clinic where we pleaded with women to not have an abortion while also sharing the gospel.

DISCUSSIONS:

Heather: Oh my god. How dare you insert yourself into someone's personal, hard-made, medical decision? That is between the woman and the doctor. It is not your place to invade such a private space and shove your personal beliefs into their digestive tracts. Disagree all you want, but you crossed a solid line. Your religious freedom ends at the next person's personal space; period, end of story. Your personal convictions are not everyone's, and you have to know by now that trying to force-feed your ideas to others ends in anger and a massive amount of disrespected feelings.

Travis Rogers: If it's not a human life, why is it such a hard decision? The fact that it's a difficult decision for so many shows that their consciences have already betrayed them. Therefore, if they know it's a human life that they're consigning to death, no amount of doctor-patient confidentiality will compensate for cold blooded murder of their own child...a human life their conscience has already convicted them of. That's no longer medicine. It's a butcher shop. I stand firm that there are absolutely zero logical and consistent arguments to be made as to why abortion should be legal. I've invited many to try and not one has been successful. It doesn't even require touching on religion in order to be a voice for the voiceless. All it takes is compassion for the child who is about to be killed and heartfelt desire for the mother to make the right decision. If it weren't a child being killed, it would be a moot point. However, since it absolutely is, anything else becomes an excuse and the issue remains critical.

At risk of sounding like I'm rambling or ranting, I did want to touch on the statement that the abortionist is a doctor. Just based on the Hippocratic Oath alone (admittedly nonbinding but still highly revered among doctors as the golden standard), the abortionist has violated his own sworn responsibility. Here is a snippet of the oath:

"I will use treatment to help the sick according to my ability and judgment, but I will never use it to injure or wrong them. I will not give poison to anyone though asked to do so, nor will I suggest such a plan. Similarly I will not give a pessary to a woman to cause abortion. But in purity and in holiness I will guard my life and my art."[i]

Abortion isn't helping the sick. It's killing the innocent. This is clearly an injury to the innocent that the real doctor swears not to perform. He also swears not to give poison to anybody when asked to do so. Yet, that's the very first step of an abortion. They poison the baby. Lastly, he swears not to cause an abortion. I find that particular line very powerful. The abortionist forsakes literally EVERY part of the Hippocratic Oath with the exception of the part about confidentiality. If this man or woman is to be called a doctor, they are a poor one at best as they have violated every ethical principle that real doctors swear to uphold.

Steven: Further to that, there is the physiological and psychological damage to the woman on whom the abortion is being performed on: The violent act of abortion can grossly harm the woman's uterus making it difficult to have a successful pregnancy later in her life; secondly, the harm to the woman's psyche can be extremely problematic to her mental health. To use *Heather's* words, "hard-made..." decision, could that be because she may be aware (deep down perhaps) that what she is doing is wrong?

Heather: Yes, religion WAS brought into it due to your reasoning and bible quotes. Your religion and personal beliefs do NOT belong in some else's bedroom or medical decisions. Unless you went there to offer to adopt their unwanted children, you were wrong. You may as well have gone to a mental health clinic and preached the dangers of psychoactive and other medications used to control the illness, citing the harmful side effects you are currently leaning on like a shoddily made crutch.

Travis Rogers: First, It's not harassment if we're simply talking with them and pleading with them to not end the life of their child. That's called responsibility.

Second, religion was brought into it in here because it shouldn't have surprised me how much hate was shown to people who simply wanted to talk. Yes, some were preaching the gospel (as they should be doing). Personally, I just wanted to talk with people and hear how they could possibly be logically consistent with their stance (of which I already know they aren't because abortion defies logic).

Third, I already covered how what they were having performed is not a medical decision. There's nothing medical about killing your child. It's a complete misnomer that's used to make people feel better about their actions.

Fourth, we had literature with us that could've pointed them in the right direction and we could've gladly been there to support them emotionally through the process. However, one doesn't need to personally offer to adopt a child in order to try to prevent a mother from killing him/her simply because they don't want him/her. Abortion is currently the leading cause of murder. It's not even close. Just because our society has deemed it legal doesn't mean it's not still murder by definition. It also doesn't make it right just because it's legal (think legal slavery in America or the Holocaust in Germany).

Fifth, your argument of mental health is comparing apples to oranges. If the side effect of someone taking medication was the 100% guaranteed death of their child (or any person for that matter), I'd be against it. However, negative side effects are simply weighted choices when compared to positive outcomes. This isn't the case with abortion as no amount of positive outcome can outweigh the 100% guaranteed side effect of the death of your own baby. Further, because the death of your baby is the intent, it's not even a side effect. The side effect would be your own pleasure, freedom of responsibility, etc. Again, apples to oranges.

What I'm curious about is why, while I'm consistently bringing the conversation back to the subject of life, you keep referring to peripheral issues. I think whether or not the fetus is life and what our responsibility is in relation to that fact should be primary. Anything else is secondary.

Heather: It's legal. Harassment is not. Plain and simple.

Travis Rogers: Do you appreciate the first Amendment of our Constitution? And, again, being legal doesn't make it right. Would you have said those speaking out against slavery were harassing others and that they should've remained silent? How about those speaking out against the Holocaust? Should they have remained quiet?

Heather: Slavery is illegal because it enables the oppression of human beings. Abortion is legal because it is a medical procedure, nondiscriminatory, and literally affects no one other than those directly involved. Abortion is as personal a choice as medication, procedures to control a condition, and going to a women's health clinic with the only intent of berating women for a personal choice is legally harassment. Even 'responsibly pleading' is unwanted, and therefore harassment.

Travis Rogers: When do you believe life begins? Are you saying abortion doesn't negatively affect the person being killed? I'd say it's very oppressive to that person. Again, when do you say life begins?

Heather: Life begins in the womb. Sentient life begins at birth. Abortion is a means to solve a problem. How many women can afford prenatal appointments? Do you know of any organizations that will take on that cost, and the cost of extra food? And financially compensate for work days missed during and after birth? And please don't say "Medicaid" or their healthcare insurance or WIC/food stamps. Medicaid, WIC and food stamps are looked down upon as "mooching" by every conservative ever, and you have to be d*** near eating dirt to qualify. Even with only $2000 a month in income, my family of four didn't qualify. Also, how many adoption programs do you know of willing to take on that kind of load at $30,000-50,000 and up per adoption for the prospective parent? Who can afford that? Or do you expect the new mother to drop her newborn off at a fire station and add more stress to an already overloaded foster system?

To me, this is an issue of quality of life for both the mother and child. The mother will suffer financially, emotionally, and physically, carrying a child she doesn't intend to keep, and the child's quality of life in poverty will be even lower, then statistically lead to lower success in school and less ability to contribute to society in a meaning way that breaks the cycle of poverty. All of this is intertwined.

Donald: *Heather* It's better to be dead than poor?

Monica: *Heather* Unfortunately, making a comment here is like talking to a brick wall as it is seen from their side as well. I practically stopped commenting on these types of topics and instead will only add my voice to causes I believe in. Voting is one way but online opposing opinions are nothing but asking for a fight these days.

Randy: *Monica* I agree. I see both sides. But this will never be a topic you can just have a conversation about and change someone's mind. It's a topic of belief not opinion. And I'd never expect to change someone's beliefs by pushing my own. Humanity just doesn't work like that.

Travis Rogers: *Randy* Why do you feel it's strictly an opinionated topic? I've found the only people who claim that are those who refuse to appeal to logic and would rather appeal to emotion.

Missy: Here's my take. If you're willing to stand up for the unborn child while still in the womb ,then hold up that same stance when it's born, grows up. What if the child is gay/transgender would you still protect that same child you protected when he/she were about to be aborted? Don't just be pro birth. Stand up for that child and that child's right to live here free in America. As long as the child is committing no crimes. Being gay/ lesbian/ transgender is not a crime. Also, if doctors would let women get their tubes tied instead of having them wait until their 30's, it would help prevent unwanted pregnancies. It's easier for a man to get a vasectomy than for a woman to get a tubal ligation.

Travis Rogers: *Missy*, nobody here is arguing to kill gay people. However, I'm not following your comment on tube tying.

What does the ability or inability to get one's tubes tied have to do with whether or not it should be legal to kill your children?

Missy: *Travis Rogers* I was just trying to bring up another point of view. I wasn't saying people here were trying to kill gay people and I'm sorry if I gave that impression off. I was just saying that if someone is pro-life that it should extend beyond the womb as in protecting the child rights after its birth. Meaning if the child is anything other than straight, its rights should still be protected. Maybe I was generalizing and did not mean to. Also, follow me here. Sex is a biological thing that humans will do regardless of some of the consequences. To prevent unwanted pregnancies women should be allowed by medical professionals to have a tubal ligation even if she wants one at 20 years old. That's not the case. Doctors won't approve the procedure unless the women has reached her 30's (with no children) or if the woman already has children. I feel it's about preventing this situation. I know there is birth control which is hard on a woman's body as well as not completely effective. Men have easier access if they choose to have a vasectomy. In addition, this country needs to get serious about sexual education and being responsible about ones sex life.

Randy: *Travis Rogers* I'm saying it's not a matter of opinion. It's a matter of belief. When do you believe life starts? Do you believe abortion is justified? Do you believe abortion is murder or mercy in rape victim cases? These aren't as simple as what's your opinion when it comes to someone else's life. I'm not disagreeing with anything you've posted on this topic. Just stating it's almost impossible to change someone's beliefs just by talking about them.

Donald: This is not just a 'different strokes for different folks' issue. Most of us against abortion are saying that it is a morally reprehensible act because it defies God's law. No amount of logic or reason will convince some otherwise because their foolish heart is darkened. Therefore, Christians will preach the Gospel because it has the power to change hearts and save unborn children.

Randy: exactly, except you don't need God to know it's wrong.

Donald: If you don't believe in God, you'd have a hard time explaining why it's wrong.

Travis Rogers: While I agree that someone who doesn't believe in God has no absolute standard about morality (after all, how does an advanced form of sludge have morals?), I think that's for a separate discussion or, at a minimum, a different thread in this discussion. As for belief that it's wrong, it's more than that. If it's a human life, it's a human life. Therefore, to justify it is to either promote or, at a minimum, condone the mass genocide of children. This is a hole that nobody wants to jump into let alone try to climb out of. Thus, they replace harsh sounding reality with softer terms, reject logic and instead appeal to emotion, and derail the conversation from one of what to do with living children into secondary and tertiary issues or excuses. It's hard to face the facts but it still needs to be done. Our culture is so inept when it comes to discussing these issues because they've grown up being told they're things we just don't talk about.

Randy: You'll have an even harder time telling someone who doesn't believe in God it's wrong because it defies God's law. I agree completely with everything you just said. Except for the no absolute standard part. But that's for a different conversation on a different page.

Travis Rogers: While it's definitely difficult to prove the bible by using the bible with someone who doesn't believe in the bible (or proving morals by using a God someone doesn't believe in), it's actually pretty simple to prove that absolute morals don't exist without God as they become a shifting standard that was created by fallible man yet not subscribed to by all. Since no man has the authority to dictate an absolute moral code, it becomes impossible to discern right from wrong. Only an absolute God can dictate absolute moral standards. Everything else becomes nothing more than accepted common opinion of what is good or bad without actually having anything to objectively base it off of. But, again, that's for another thread.

As for this topic, it's either life or it isn't. If it isn't, there's no argument nor should there be any difficult decisions to be made. It's simply throwing out the daily trash. Have 50 abortions and then shoot for 100 if that's your prerogative. However, if it is indeed life (as all science and medicine point to the affirmative), it has to be dealt with in absolute standards as it becomes absolute legal murder and the slaughtering of innocent lives.

---

[i] The hippocratic oath. (1998). BMJ : British Medical Journal, 317(7166), 1110.

Example #6

OPENING STATEMENT:

Travis Rogers: Why is it that those who call themselves AHA Abortion Abolitionists are aligning themselves with the pro-abortion crowd in condemning the Heartbeat Bills?

CONTEXT:

Article with a headline stating, "Ohio State Senate Passes One of America's Most Restrictive Abortion Bills." The bill calls for banning abortion if a heartbeat is detected via an ultrasound. Heartbeats can be detected as early as six weeks. Proponents feel this is a step in the right direction. Opponents (to include abortion abolitionists) feel this bill is evil since a heartbeat is easy to 'miss' if you don't want one to be found. The pro-life responses below are justifying incremental legislation while the abolitionists are condemning it.

DISCUSSIONS:

Sasha: Abolitionists are against regulating murder. These bills dishonor God and break His commandments.

Travis Rogers: AHA believes, since a heartbeat can be easily missed on purpose and the abortion would go forward, it's a garbage bill that should be rejected. However, what they fail to see is that, if it saves even one life, it's well worth getting a foot in the door. The "go big or go home" mentality will only serve to allow more babies to be needlessly murdered whereas, if we took our wins where we can get them, even if in the form of baby steps (pun intended), we may just incrementally save lives. It's like the old saying goes, "How do you eat an elephant? One bite at a time."

Christopher: *Travis Rogers* The issue is not save some babies/no babies/ all babies. The issue is whether the law is just or unjust. The issue is: Does the law show sinful partiality or not?

Sasha: *Travis Rogers* It actually keeps abortion going. Therefore more lives ended. If we had put forth and supported a total abolition bill instead, that would be God-honoring and baby murder would actually come to a screeching halt in Ohio. Plus, ever think about why "this is the best of what we can get?" Maybe because that's all pro-lifers are asking for.

Travis Rogers: *Sasha* Look at the world we live in. I can tell you a bill like that simply wouldn't pass at this point in time. It's a pipe dream and pretending it isn't is only costing babies their lives. However, what is absolutely possible is going for a quick win that will potentially save countless lives and then continuing to make forward movement toward the ultimate goal of abortion being illegal as a whole.

Theodore: *Travis Rogers* Regulatory bills that continue to surrender the only real moral, constitutional, and legal argument against abortion on demand, which is equal protection under the law for the supreme God-given unalienable human right, will never "save some" as their utilitarian promoters constantly suggest. In fact, they assure the continuation of abortion on demand.

Saban: *Sasha* But lives are being saved. But you're not satisfied at all and never will be. That is the attitude of the AHA advocate. According to you, we should reject the Bill and let babies get murdered. Doesn't make sense on your end and sorry, if the heartbeat bill is going to save lives, I'm all in. Do we stop there? Absolutely not! We continue to fight toward our goal of ending abortion if the Lord permits, which is also God-honoring. You sure love to criticize pro-lifers but what if your so called honoring bill goes through (which I'm all for it) and it fails, and then we send the heartbeat bill and it passes? You would still not be satisfied and will blame pro-lifers for failing on their part, instead of praising God for His mercy and grace through this bill that will save lives.

Luther: *Travis Rogers,* and it is much better to sacrifice other children in the name of a nebulous empty bill, eh?

Saban: *Theodore* Are lives being saved? Answer yes or no. Thank you.

Theodore: No. It's a mirage.

Christopher: And unjust.

Saban: *Theodore* How do you know? Because it will save lives. That is a long stretch to say it is a mirage.

Theodore: It can't save any lives when it keeps surrendering the only moral, constitutional, and legal argument against abortion on demand. It's not possible. The bill is intrinsically immoral and unconstitutional. That's what you utilitarians either don't get, or don't care about. The big irony is that in the end it's also not utile. Ever.

Saban: If lives were not saved then I agree with you. But they are being saved and you're refusing to acknowledge that, which is fine. We all have presuppositions coming into this. I understand, but the reality is babies lives are being saved whether you disagree with the bill or not. This is the mercy of God on our nation. This is what me and my friend were discussing about earlier this week. Lives are being saved.

Theodore: You can't prove that babies are being saved, because only God knows how many are being murdered. It's nothing but a baseless utilitarian claim that can't be proved.

Travis Rogers: *Theodore* By your logic, you can't prove how many babies are being murdered because only God knows how many are being saved. By your own logic, you must now support the bill and fight anyone who thinks all babies are being murdered and none are being saved. You see how illogical your premise is?

Justin: The OP is dishonest. We are against the heartbeat bills because they are wicked, nearly impossible to implement and do not seek to apply equal justice. Christians shouldn't support them at all. The pro-choice folks condemn such bills because they create an obstacle for women to have freedom to murder their children.

Travis Rogers: I'm okay with obstacles. Especially if it saves even one life.

Justin: What if in supporting the obstacle, you have to disobey the word of God? Are you still okay with it?

Jason: *Justin* Isn't it a shame the Civil War was incrementalist? They could have fought not just for an end to slavery so men who were slaves would have an equal vote, but for women as well. Since so many people died only for one group of people to acquire the proper acknowledgement of their rights and not others, I guess the Civil War was a waste. Female slaves would have to wait even longer for their rights.

Travis Rogers: *Justin* The problem with your question is that it's a false premise. The law already allows for abortion. In some states, up until birth. In others, even after birth. Fighting to make certain cases illegal isn't synonymous with fighting to keep other instances legal. Those would be legal regardless. It's a fight to whittle away at immorality little by little while saving as many lives as possible incrementally.

Jason: I see people who use both approaches in pro-life efforts offering value. We should strive for the full protection of life from conception. However, people fall all over a wide range of views on the subject when one looks at the general population. I would love to see

118

everyone see the value in life from the beginning. But some people get there by being nudged from a deeply held position to something in the middle. Then as the views that deceived them before continue to fall away, they find themselves able to go even more in the pro-life direction. If someone can make the jump all at once, that is great. But it seems like people are expecting everyone to flip like a switch to a stance that most of society considers extreme, no matter how reasonable it is.

Travis Rogers: *Jason* That's essentially what I'm getting at. You just put it much better. You're right when you say that we've seen the "nothing" for too long. Essentially, it's saying the relative few lives that may be saved can just go ahead and die because they're holding out for the big win. Either they're going to save everybody or nobody. It's absolutely foolish, in my opinion.

Tara: *Travis Rogers* Save all lives or no lives? That makes no sense. I am an Abolitionist. If we cannot Abolish Abortion in obedience to our Creator because of incremental regulated abortions under the Pro Life movement, then we aren't saving 'no lives'. That is a lie. If the pro-life incrementalists get their way and 62 more million babies die in the next 45 years then their blood will not be on our hands, because we tried to obey the Lord. Saying that we want all babies to die if we don't win is absurd.

Saban: *Tara* What you just said makes no sense. If you reject this bill that will save a lot of lives then aren't you disobeying your Creator by not seeing this is God's Sovereignty, His mercy and grace toward our nation? How are lives not being saved through incremental bills? Have you checked to see if that is accurate or are you making a claim that you cannot verify? I don't think that's not fair. And if we go with your way then no lives will be saved at all, but you will quickly blame the Christian pro-life for failing.

Tara: Why not pass an Abolition Bill? We have had 45 years of Pro Life Bills. We can abolish abortion if we can get the Pro Life people to join us. Why do they fight us? They fight us tooth and nail. That is what makes no sense.

Justin: No, lives are not being saved. You've been sold a bill of goods. *Jason* while I appreciate your replies, I simply disagree with the foundation of your argument. I don't believe these bills save lives, I believe they are unjust according to the word of God and I believe incremental steps that have been applied over the last 40 years by the pro-life movement have gotten us absolutely nothing but millions of dead babies. This is all pretty simple. The standard in which we measure success is different. The pro-life movement seeks to save lives no matter the cost and the abolitionists seek to stand on the word of God and measure success by obedience to His Word. We must obey God rather than men.

Travis Rogers: *Justin* Here's a quick question for you. If the federal government would pass a bill banning all abortions except for cases of rape or incest, would you be in favor of that? Now, we both know neither rape nor incest nullify life so that's not my question. Would you be in favor of such a law being passed if it meant dropping the abortion rate down to that incredibly small percentage and saving hundreds of thousands of lives every year? If so, you support incrementalism whether you like it or not. If you wouldn't support it, it shows you care more about seeing laws change exactly how you want them to (i.e. winning a war regardless of how much collateral damage it takes) than you do saving innocent lives. There you have it. If the former, this entire thread is null and void. However, if the latter, it speaks volumes. Additionally, you keep saying we're being unfaithful to the Word of God but I have yet to see you justify your claims from Scripture.

Justin: No, I would not be in favor of it. And the defense of my position can be summed up in 3 words. God is just.

Travis Rogers: Then my point is made. You'd rather fight a war even if it costs millions of lives in the process, instead of gaining ground little by little and saving untold numbers of victims in the process. God is just but, according to the babies who will die at the hand of your stubbornness, you are not.

Justin: Again, justice is not measured by how many lives are saved by supporting a wicked law. Justice is measured by the word of God. We disagree. I appreciate the dialogue.

Travis Rogers: I absolutely love the dialogue. If we can't speak civilly (even if passionately) on our disagreements, all hope is lost. The biggest problem I see with the abolitionist position is that it places an emphasis on policy over person. It seeks to abolish policy and replace it with more policy instead of saving lives. It wants to defeat evil more than it wants to perform good. It wants to win a war more than it wants to save the innocent. In all honesty, in my opinion, it's more administrative fanaticism based in a vision of utopia than it is fighting in the trenches hoping to gain as much ground as possible until the war is won. One side is political in an ivory tower while the other side actually cares about human lives. Our goal is to save lives with the end game being the abolishing of abortion, whereas the abolitionist is more focused on abolishing policy no matter how many lives are lost in the process. That's not justice.

Justin: I would encourage you to look into the abolitionist position. You seem to not understand what we represent and it has caused you to attack a strawman. I say this respectfully, this is a common problem within the pro-life community.

Travis Rogers: There's nothing to misrepresent. It's the logical conclusion of your position. If a bill will potentially save the life of another, you consider it wicked since it allows the rest to go unchecked. However, it refuses to acknowledge the fact that our ultimate goal is to make it all illegal in due process. On the flip side, the abolitionist feels self-righteous and vindicated claiming they are doing the Lord's work by continuing to fight for all lives at once even if it means saving none. Oddly enough, both sides turn to God's sovereignty. The pro-life side appeals to God's sovereign grace in the means of incremental laws that progressively save more and more lives. The abolitionist side appeals to God's sovereignty to justify why their position hasn't saved anyone. Incremental legislation has saved more lives than the zero that the abolitionist movement has saved. Those are the numbers. Again, we don't have to like the darkness but we can't pretend it doesn't exist or delude ourselves into thinking a secular society of lawmakers are going to eradicate abortion in the blink of an eye. It's just not profitable. But, hey, as long as you can feel self-righteous in knowing you want them to live, keep bashing those who are *actually* saving lives every day.

Connor: *Travis Rogers* Because they believe it's better to save no children if you can't save all of them.

Luther: *Connor*, whereas you believe that it's okay to kill some babies.

Connor: Not at all. That's why I argue against abortion and try to convince people that abortion is wrong. By supporting a heartbeat bill, it is not in any sense saying that it is okay to kill babies before that point. Even Planned Parenthood recognizes them as incremental steps to chip away at *Roe v. Wade*.

Tara: *Connor* I don't believe it's better to save no children if we can't save them all. We can compromise and work together. Join us in passing an Abolition bill and if that doesn't pass then I will know I did what God commands me to do and I will accept some saved instead of all saved. I would never say kill them all. That's not a valid argument.

Connor: *Tara* Join us in passing incremental bills, and you'll know that you are doing the Lord's work. The Lord has said nothing about what type of legislation we ought to support. God hasn't commanded you to do anything other than be faithful and stand up for the oppressed. To allow all children to die because you can't save them all is what is really evil. Saving what lives we can save is what we should be doing.

Theodore: *Connor*, you say, "By supporting a heartbeat bill, it is not in any sense saying that it is okay to kill babies before that point." But that's simply not true. The bills themselves give explicit governmental permission to kill all the babies, as long as they are killed on schedule.

Travis Rogers: *Theodore* The bill did nothing of the sort. Those laws already exist. This bill simply reduces the power of existing laws. Once culture sees that as normal, we strike again. Eventually, abortion is illegal. You know why the abortion industry is so powerful? They accepted incremental wins over the course of decades and slowly indoctrinated the culture. They didn't just go from abortion being illegal straight to demanding partial birth abortion. They played the long game because they knew it was the only way they'd get it to pass. They've been doing this longer than we have so we need to use their playbook against them.

Richard: *Travis Rogers* The "prolife" movement has spent nearly 50 years compromising with murderers and thieves. There can be no justice when we are willing to allow them to kill "just a few." Where is your sense of justice for THEM?

Travis Rogers: *Richard* What's more important to you: policy change or saved lives? Obviously, the ultimate goal is policy change that saves lives but, if there could be only one, which is it? I'm not living in a pipe dream that deludes myself into thinking we're going to miraculously change the hearts and minds of a wicked people in a single instant. To think a total abolitionist bill will be made into law is about as asinine as thinking abortion got to the place we're currently at overnight. It took time, increments, and patience while pushing an agenda and slowly indoctrinating a culture to include their children. So,

I ask again, which is more important to you? Are you in this to save lives or are you in this to effect policy and legislation? Part of the reason it's taken so long to effect change is because abolitionists vote against bills that would've been a huge incremental step in the right direction. As such, we go right back to square one while the abolitionist blames the pro-life movement. In reality, it's the abolitionist who is directly contributing to the murder of children by refusing to save even one. We don't have to like the fact that children will still be murdered under incremental laws, and we don't have to stop pursuing more change, but we should all be able to feel thankful for the multitude of children who may not have to die any longer. Remember, these are real people we're fighting for, not simply policy.

Example #7

OPENING STATEMENT:

Elise: Should abortion be legal?

CONTEXT:

In a poll asking whether abortion should be legal, a person commented with the below statement and shared a list of various crimes against humanity, one of which stated, "forced pregnancy."

DISCUSSIONS:

Elise: Just so we're clear, you can dislike abortions ALLLLL you want, but forced birth/pregnancy is literally a crime against humanity.

Travis Rogers: And what about the crime against humanity in the removal of the life of another against their will? Forcing someone to get pregnant is certainly a crime but nobody is arguing for that to be legal.

Elise: A fetus' right to life stops where my body begins just as everyone else's does. I'm under no obligation to give up ANY part of me to sustain the life of another. Period. Forcing someone to carry a baby is literally a crime.

Travis Rogers: You're taking loose wording and assigning your own definition. The picture you posted said forced pregnancy. It said nothing about forced carry. As I stated earlier, impregnating someone by force is highly illegal. However, once pregnant, carrying is simply a natural bodily response. It's autonomous. There's a huge difference between forced pregnancy and forced carrying. Again, all we're saying is someone shouldn't have the right to purposefully kill another human being against their will.

Elise: What the h***? No, that's just one way to look at it. Forced pregnancy means the entire pregnancy, not how it occurred.

Travis Rogers: Says you. I read it otherwise. How can you say my interpretation is wrong but yours is right? I'd argue your definition is simply out of context.

Elise: No one has the right to kill another human being against their will. That is murder, something abortion isn't.

Travis Rogers: From conception, it's a human being at a varying stage of development in the human life cycle. This is basic biology that isn't even argued anymore among serious critics of the pro-life movement.

Elise: I guess so. Regardless, abortion ≠ murder. I never denied it being human. Literally ever. It. Is. Not. A L I V E. I don't understand why y'all can't grasp this. I've repeated it so many times.

Travis Rogers: Nobody argued murder. I said purposeful killing. Murder is a legal term. While abortion fits the general idea of murder, our legal system doesn't constitute it as such. That said, regardless whether the legal system recognizes it or not, it remains the purposeful and forceful taking of human life. If it became legal tomorrow to kill your neighbor, it'd no longer be murder but it's still a killing.

Elise: How can you kill or take the life of something with no life to speak of?

Travis Rogers: So, you say it's a human (by saying you're not denying my statement that it is) but also said abortion isn't the killing of a human. Thus, the only logical conclusion is that the human in the womb is dead and then comes to life (since the only two states of humans are either dead or alive). However, this isn't scientific.

Elise: I said it's not killing at all. Abortion stops it from growing and expels it. It's not alive until it has a consciousness and around 20+ weeks. Abortions are no longer performed unless medically necessary.

Travis Rogers: I think you need to go through and read some recent laws. In fact, New York's law seriously removed any restrictions. That's not me regurgitating internet stories. I literally read the entire law while comparing it to the previous one. Additionally, plants don't have a consciousness, yet they're still deemed to be alive. Consciousness doesn't have anything to do with whether something is alive or not. Sensory response or the ability to possess cognition are indicators of life but aren't what defines it.

Brenda: A woman is pregnant from conception? How do y'all reconcile that with 86% of fertilized eggs that don't implant? Are those little people being flushed on a tampon?

Travis Rogers: That's exactly right. It's sad but it's scientific. From the moment of fertilization, a unique genetic code with the little human's entire life already mapped out (to include predispositions) is created. That's the fundamental code of life. Whether that life implants, live, or dies is another story altogether.

(The original author deleted her post and the entire thread along with it so further discussion was no longer possible)

Example #8

OPENING STATEMENT:

Travis Rogers: None of the pro-choice side chatter really adds up to anything. Here's why:

1) They argue rape/incest should be legal justification to obtain abortion.

2) They argue the fetus isn't a person until much later in the pregnancy.

3) They argue that foster children are ignored.

4) They argue that the mother's life may be at stake.

5) They argue it's forcing women into a financial burden.

Yet, if a bill were put forth stating rape/incest was justification, early term abortion was legal, adopting and fostering would become easy as pie, a mother's life being at stake is justification, and all their baby's financial needs would be covered by the government, they'd still argue against it. Thus, it proves absolutely none of those points really matter to them because they'll accept nothing less than abortion on demand for any reason at any time.

End conclusion: If you're not willing to concede your position once the other side has conceded to your arguments and demands, they really aren't arguments you believe in or feel anything for. They're just hollow talking points because you have nothing substantial to actually say.

CONTEXT:

The pro-choice community has created many excuses as to why abortion should be legal but none of them matter because, even if concessions were made, they'd still want it legal.

DISCUSSIONS:

Harry: I've seen no such concessions from the anti-choice party. Have you?

Travis Rogers: Anti-choice is a misnomer. Pro-lifers greatly appreciate choice. We just don't think anyone should have the choice to murder their kid. As for the concessions, some have been around for decades and the pro-murder party still wants more. Remember, it's that party that keeps bringing up those arguments, not pro-lifers. Do you deny that the pro-choicers won't be happy even if they were all met?

Donald: *Harry* Abstinence, contraception, motherhood, adoption. There are many choices, just not cool with murder.

Harry: "Pro-life" is a misnomer which does not seem universally true for those who use that term. Not to mention a "fetus" does not equate to "their kid" based on their own beliefs. All of those arguments are still secondary to the core belief of "her body, her choice." I can't speak for everyone on the pro-choice side, but I'm certain that a percentage of them would feel better if these concessions were actually offered, but this post implies some sort of proof under circumstances that don't exist. The right has been working to increase restrictions on choice, never the opposite.

Harry: *Donald* Murder is a legal term. If it's legal it's not murder. And very few Americans can make the claim they don't support killing under circumstances of their own choice. But the reality is, what you believe is a life, others do not. This fundamental debate is buried by making claims that ignore it like this. Unless everyone agrees that it's "life" we can't really debate death.

Tabitha: Science has proven it is life though. That's a garbage tactic, sorry. The baby develops a heartbeat at 16 days old, 16 days after having implanted. The cells have already so clearly defined a functioning heart that it is visible on ultrasound, and women can SEE this at their 6-8 week ultrasound. (Sooner if their doctors can manage to fit them in, most can't.) So the thought this ISN'T a life is complete and utter garbage. American bald eagles still in the egg are protected to the point that it's illegal to kill an unhatched egg because it's obviously recognized that it's a life inside there. Shall I continue? Post articles backed by verified scientific evidence that you won't read?

Travis Rogers: *Harry*, I've heard the claim that murder is only a legal term and, thus, can't be used by the pro-life crowd. However, that's not entirely correct. While there is a legal definition, to include varying degrees, there is also the use of the word as a verb. You're merely identifying the noun. As a verb, it stands independent of legal jargon. As for your claim that her choice is superior to the argument of fetal life, I wholeheartedly disagree. Due to the principle of non-aggression, a person is free to act within their own choices but may not commit an act of aggression toward another. Thus, putting personal freedom over the safety of another by either committing or condoning an act of aggression toward another would be considered unethical at its very core. Now, you may not agree with that ethical position within this debate but I'm pretty sure you'd agree with it if someone were to try to kill you in your sleep and someone could do something to stop it from happening.

Harry: *Travis Rogers* I expected that you would wholeheartedly disagree. If I shared your belief, my stance would be the same. I don't believe that a fetus, until a certain point, is a person. I get that you do, and I actually respect your will to defend them. But we don't agree that it constitutes death of a human being. Arguments based on that premise are not effective for those who don't agree with it. This wasn't supposed to be another endless debate over opinions. I just asked when, where, or who has made concessions from the pro-life side that gives any merit to the assertion made in the original post. Nobody has answered that question, only reverted to the stale arguments of their personal beliefs that everyone has already heard.

Harry: *Tabitha* The biologic definition of life may apply to a fetus, but does it constitute human life? Feel free to share any scientific articles with me. I would in fact read them. As a reminder the science, according to most, is settled on climate change, too. Yet, not everyone supports those findings. Strangely, there is a huge overlap in the pro-life crowd and the anti-climate-science crowd. It seems they can be selective as to what science they embrace.

Travis Rogers: *Harry*, my point was in stating that the concessions, while some have been made (i.e. late term distinctions, life of mother, rape/incest, etc), none of them really mattered. This is because the pro-choice side doesn't want concessions. They want it all. Therefore, their argument about all of those points is useless and doesn't have any intrinsic or inherent value because they don't even believe in it themselves. They don't really want those concessions. They just want to argue as if they do because it keeps them talking. In reality, I have far more respect for those who don't try to argue points they don't even believe in and are just honest about what they really want instead. As for personhood, while we could debate that all day long, it really is irrelevant as that's just another legal term. In fact, Amazon is recognized as a U.S. person but a prenatal child who has only 30 seconds until birth currently is not. This is pretty backwards. No, instead, we can argue about humanity. Your reply seems to value human life, just not all of it.

Harry: You have doubled down on the assertion that when given concessions, the pro-choice group doesn't actually value them. That's probably true for some, but a pretty broad generalization. Still absent though is the fulfillment of my request for an example. Perhaps I have missed something, but I don't recall any concessions offered in any proposals by the right. If you have some examples, then I would be forced to reconsider my lack of support for this argument.

Travis Rogers: I made them and then repeated them. Consistent pro-lifers want complete abolition of abortion. There have been several concessions offered that have all been met with resistance and vehemence from the pro-choice community. Some direct examples are:

1) Heartbeat bills. Essentially, if there's a discernable heartbeat, you can't kill the child. If not, you still can.

2) Late term abortion bans. In other words, allowing abortion up to a certain point but not beyond except in the case of life endangerment.

3) Rape/incest. Most places allow abortion in those cases.

4) Life endangerment. In cases where the mother may die, abortion is allowed.

5) Waiting periods. So long as she waits the waiting period in order to have time to think about it, she can have one.

I don't like any if those options but, regardless, they're still concessions that have been offered in order to lower abortion rates via law while not going total abolition. Even with these (and many more I didn't list), the pro-choice community refuses to accept it and, instead, finds new excuses and hollow points just to keep the chatter going. Again, this is because they don't want concessions or common ground. They want their way with no excuses or consequences.

Harry: If there was a Bill to make abortion illegal, but with these caveats attached, that was voted on, just share the bill number so we can see the language and count the votes. What Bill was this? You called these "direct examples" but they are not very direct. Who offered these concessions, who declined them? The heartbeat Bills are not concessions, they are a ban under certain criteria that prohibits nearly all abortion. They do not have any concessions in them. We should remove that from your list of examples.

Travis Rogers: If it compromises the position of abolition, it's a concession. Remember, the pro-life position argues that life starts at conception. The pro-choice argument is that it doesn't. Therefore, if pro-lifers compromise on that point, that's called a concession. It's practically textbook concession. As for the bills, Google them. They're readily available. Regarding your comment that a fetus is life but not human life, that pretty much violates all science. If something is alive, it remains in its genus for the remainder of its life. There's no such thing as crossing over. Homo is the genus that encompasses all humans. Thus, if my genus is homo, it was also that way when I was living life as a fetus.

Harry: That's not a concession, that's just a position change. It doesn't concede a point made by the opposition. They don't believe the heartbeat is the determining factor. If a flat-earther suddenly said "ok, fine the earth is hexagonal." Is that a concession, and to whom? You might be a better googler than me, I'm not finding any bills that fit this description. Perhaps you could just share the ones that you read, which were the basis for this post.

Travis Rogers: There's zero position change involved. The pro-lifer still wants complete abolition. The pro-choicer wants complete and utter freedom to abort on demand for any reason at any time. Therefore, if the pro-lifer still stands behind abolition but makes a concession for various instances, that's the textbook example. Neither side has shifted their position, just the ground their trying to claim. I'd have to Google links for you. I don't exactly keep things bookmarked. For starters, I've already well established why heartbeat bills are concessions and not merely position changes. The rest have been longstanding exceptions to ban bills but they've been fought against by pro-choicers seeking to gain more ground. I also find it hard to believe you've never seen a bill that allowed for it in cases of mother endangerment. In fact, the heartbeat bills have this built into them. Seriously, if you didn't see them, either you didn't look or you don't accept what you found as concessions.

Harry: I have seen them. But I don't see them as concessions because it's already legal. It's just a slightly less restrictive ban. I do recognize it as a form of compromise, which is good I suppose, but not concessions. I see why you feel I am wrong, I don't need to push any further. I do appreciate your willingness to have a rational discussion about it with me. I can only respect that.

Travis Rogers: I'm all about rational discussions. Even if things get heated or passionate, displaying mutual respect is always the end goal as far as I'm concerned. Nobody ever won somebody over by belittling them.

Example #9

OPENING STATEMENT:

Travis Rogers: For those who say only late term abortions should be illegal, answer this:

What exactly is late term? Is it the baby's ability to survive outside of the womb? Is that strictly unassisted or are they allowed medical assistance? If the former, are we now free to slaughter premature born babies and those with respiratory machines and pacemakers? If the latter, at what point is it life? After all, a baby in New York City (where medical care is top notch) has a much stronger chance at survival than say a home birth in a small village of Africa. Does access to elite medical service now dictate who deserves to live and die? I'm hoping you, the reader, see how this one exception, while stated by many, doesn't really hold water when logically scrutinized.

CONTEXT:

The term viability holds very little meaning when it comes to pregnancy and abortion.

DISCUSSIONS:

Estefan: You're seriously a f***ing idiot (ad hominem, just so you know.) A fetus is not viable, no matter how many machines you connect it to, for the first 1/2 of pregnancy and only 20-35% viable at 24 weeks. I'd say that's a pretty f***ing important fact, and one that most states use to establish limits for abortion. If life does start at conception, should we start charging mothers who have miscarriages with homicide? I mean, after all, it's obviously the mother's fault that she miscarried and she should be held accountable, right? Your misguided opinions on reproductive rights clearly come from religious indoctrination. What does it say that a loving God (whichever you happen to believe in) would let an innocent "life" die after conception due to no fault of the mother? Does a miscarriage mean God is an accessory to murder? If you think this sounds ridiculous then perhaps you should take a look at the s*** you've posted for the past week, shut the f*** up, and educate yourself on f***ing facts before spouting off about a topic that 13 year old girls clearly know more about than you do. I mean, f***, with the amount of dumb s*** you say about reproduction I'm amazed that you knew how to have children.

Travis Rogers: Way to be a class act. At least you recognize your ad hominem at this point unlike where you pretended it wasn't when you took your assault on religion and attempted to discredit someone due to being a Christian instead of actually addressing the points being presented.

Now, on to your claims. If there's only a 20-35% chance of saving you from a car accident, do they extract you from the wreckage and rush you to a hospital or do they leave that up to the personal feelings and opinions of the rescuers? Furthermore, viability is different from place to place and includes factors such as medical availability and experience. What's viable today wasn't viable 100 years ago. Does that mean those who survive today are only more human because of technology and medical breakthroughs? Medicine only saves lives. It doesn't determine or dictate it. I'd say that's a pretty important fact, one that should be used to save lives instead of destroying them.

As for addressing those who have a miscarriage, that's a Leftist fearmongering tactic. Go through the annals of history in this nation, to include when abortion was illegal, and tell me how many cases there have been where a mother was charged for spontaneous miscarriage. The answer is zero. There's zero legal precedent for it. Beyond that, charges are only ever brought to someone when ther"s sufficient evidence of a crime. Considering miscarriages happen for many reasons, including natural ones, there's almost no way to build a case against a mother who miscarries. Even if she smoked, drank, or did drugs, there's no way to definitively prove it led to the miscarriage as children are born all the time under those circumstances. Then again, I think you already knew that but figured it creates more chatter so might as well throw it out there.

As for God, since you clearly want to discuss religion, He is sovereign over all things. Since all have sinned and fallen short of His glory, we all deserve the wages of our sin: death. In Adam, sin entered into this world and all of humanity fell with him as our federal head. The good news of the gospel is that, with Christ as our federal head, all who have faith in his life, death, burial, and resurrection can see eternal life. Those who reject his Lordship will face judgment from a vengeful God when every knee shall bow and every tongue confess that Jesus Christ is Lord. But, alas, it'll be too late. Now is the time. None of us deserve His mercy as we all deserve death. But, in His kindness, He has called some unto Himself, not on the basis of our deeds but on the basis of His grace. Though we don't understand why He has orchestrated certain things to be, we can trust that He alone is righteous and that all things work together for good to those who love God.

And, just remember, you're the one who felt the need to visit my wall (apparently for the past week) just so you can spout your opinions and attempt to discredit religious people from any sort of intellectual discussion on no more grounds than simply the fact that they trust in God. Want another opinion? That's pretty sad. I'll be praying for you.

Jerry: *Estefan* Why the anger? And a few incorrect points in your post should be pointed out. By the logic you used in your position, the human race should no longer exist. If a fetus is not viable for the first half of pregnancy, then no humans would ever be born. It's only non-viable when it's removed from the womb. So that argument, which many use, is a non-starter. And please show me the medical research that proves my wife was responsible for her miscarriage. Take some of that anger you expressed in your post, and use that energy to learn actual medical facts.

According to Dr. Harry Mills, PhD., anger can be a "social emotion" brought on by pain. I have to wonder if perhaps somewhere in the dark, secret places of your conscience, you know this is a travesty of the human condition, but to admit that to yourself would be tantamount to admitting that you support genocide. So you get angry at the people that shine a light into that dark place in your conscience, because people crave darkness when their actions are wrong.

Estefan: *Jerry* seriously?! Do you not understand the term viability? There are factors other than an abortion that can lead to a fetus not being carried to term. In those instances, should we punish the woman? By your own experiences, you clearly don't think so. My post was hyperbolic on purpose to emphasize how ridiculous *Travis* has been on the topic.

Travis Rogers: *Estefan* I addressed your non-points. Feel free to do the same.

Estefan: *Travis Rogers* you are, literally, too ignorant to argue with, so I'm just going to leave this here. *(AUTHOR NOTE: URL redacted. Article was about Rennie Gibbs, Bei Bei Shuai, and Amanda Kimbrough, claiming women who lose babies are being charged with murder.)*[i] You're entitled to your own opinion but not your own facts. When you use religious values as a grounds to argue legal matters it's a slippery slope. I've already read about challenges to laws designed to restrict reproductive rights by the satanic church based on religious grounds, which only proves it cuts both ways. As I've said all along (although you've probably missed it) you can believe what you want, but you are not entitled to force others to comport to your beliefs, period.

Jerry: Viable-(of a plant, animal, or cell) capable of surviving or living successfully, especially under particular environmental conditions. A fetus is absolutely viable, if left undisturbed. To use the non-viable argument to support abortion is factually incorrect. Most, if not all, living things are non-viable when removed from their natural habitat. If I would take you and put you in the middle of Antarctica without proper clothes and shelter, you would die. Because you are "not viable" in that scenario, should I have the right to terminate you? And to carry your parallel example to the extreme, should we euthanize every person with chronic medical conditions. To compare miscarriages to abortions is intellectually dishonest and lazy. One is a spontaneous medical event and the other is a deliberate action. If that's the best argument you can make, then I understand your anger.

Travis Rogers: *Estefan* Rennie Gibbs' case was dismissed when no cocaine was found in the blood of the child. Bei Bei Shuai had a three day old child who died due to being poisoned while in the womb. At that point, nobody can deny her born child died due to her negligence (although, technically, negligence requires passivity while she actively administered poison into her child's bloodstream) while in a low emotional state. Amanda Kimbrough's baby was also born alive and died due to her actions.

See the common trend? Those who had babies who were born but then died because of the actions of the mother were charged because they caused a born child to die. Those children who were deemed to not be connected to those actions (and in that particular case weren't even born alive) were dropped upon review of the evidence. Of course, it figures a far Left biased and agenda driven media outlet would try to spin the stories to fit their narrative even if it's not honest journalism.

Furthermore, my point still stands. Not a single miscarriage in all of U.S. history has led to actual charges. The closest thing was a stillbirth where the charges were rapidly dropped after reviewing the facts. Add to it that all of those "half-truth" stories were from years prior to any of these laws changing in favor of pro-life, and it further proves my point.

---

[i] d Pilkington, "Outcry in America as pregnant women who lose babies face murder charges," *The Guardian*, June 24, 2011, https://www.theguardian.com/world/2011/jun/24/america-pregnant-women-murder-charges

Example #10

Phillip: So, Democrats don't want to fund border security yet they're fighting to fund the murder and slaughtering of innocent babies? Is there any morality left in that party?

CONTEXT:

Article with headline stating, "Pelosi, House Dems pass spending bill funding abortion; White House vows veto."[i]

DISCUSSIONS:

Phillip: That's like me saying "So Republicans want to spend billions on a border wall that could be spent on homeless veterans?"

Travis Rogers: In your example, both are beneficial and honorable subjects where a decision has to be made on what to fund first. However, in the example I gave, one is glorifying the murder of children while saying our government should fund such atrocities. How do you defend that? It's pure evil.

Phillip: If it was actually proven to be murder, that would make sense.

Travis Rogers: Considering science and medicine have proven the fetus to be life, and murder is the forceful removal of the life of another against their will, that makes sense. For those who say it's not murder, I think they choose to ignore the facts in lieu of their preferences.

Phillip: I need the sources, otherwise I don't know what I'm allegedly ignoring. To be fair, my example above is not a good comparison. I just believe differently than you about immigration (hence you being more right-leaning, and I more left-leaning).

Travis Rogers: I'm open to there being differences in opinion on immigration. Unless one goes in an extreme direction, it really doesn't get into the realm of morality (though some of the unexpected results possibly could).

Like I said above, if one looks at the situation without first viewing it through their lens of preference, it becomes pretty obvious that the fetus is a human life at an earlier stage of development in the human lifecycle. I'll try to pull some references later when I'm on my computer if it might actually sway your understanding on such a critical issue.

As an important note, people readily accept that amoebas, plants, and starfish are living organisms. Simply put, they are life. If I tried to argue this point, I'd be looked at like I were crazy, stupid, or both. Yet, though a fetus has human DNA, human cells, human traits, respond to stimuli, and slowly starts to look like a fully developed human (whatever that actually means, considering even we are still developing), people still try to argue that the fetus isn't human life. Most people aren't uninformed nor have they reached a different conclusion. I fully believe, in their heart, they know the truth. They just harden their hearts to fight against what they know to be true. Considering the consequence is a poisoned and slaughtered child, there's no other way to classify it other than pure evil of a wicked world.

---

[i] Samuel Smith, "Pelosi, House Dems pass spending bill funding abortion; White House vows veto," *The Christian Post*, January 4, 2019, https://www.christianpost.com/news/pelosi-house-democratss-pass-spending-bill-funding-abortion-white-house-vows-veto.html

Example #11

OPENING STATEMENT:

Jasmine: Well, that's interesting. Since I was 4 months pregnant in my fallopian tube and there was a heartbeat. I would've died had the doctor not aborted the pregnancy.

CONTEXT:

News article about a new South Carolina bill. The media outlet said, "The measure says abortions can't happen after a fetal heartbeat is detected."[i]

DISCUSSIONS:

Jorge: No one argues against medical exceptions.

Jasmine: Give it time.

Travis Rogers: Doubtful. All we want is for people to stop dehumanizing other human beings in the name of choice.

Jasmine: I guess that'll happen when people stop selling animals and trafficking children. There's a lot of evil in the world. But I still don't want someone controlling what goes in and out of my body. I am against abortion, but I am more against other's forcing belief's on other people. There's always going to be someone wanting bad things to go away, but if others are desperate enough, they'll commit the offense regardless. No one on this planet lives anywhere near perfect.

Travis Rogers: Have you ever asked yourself why you are against abortion? Most people who are against it is because they know killing an innocent human being is wrong. At that point, it's more than a matter of personal preference. It's literally a matter of life and death. Pro-choice means being willing to say, "It's okay to kill an innocent human being when I feel I'm no longer free to do what I want." With that in mind, why are we not free to use our bodies to stab people? Why are we not free to use our fingers to pull a trigger in a school filled with kids? It's because killing others is absolutely wrong. Telling someone they're not free to use their body in such a manner as it ends in the death of an innocent party is not synonymous with oppression or a lack of freedom.

Jasmine: I'm against it because killing is wrong, innocent or not. But that's how I feel. I'm not going to force my beliefs on someone else. Not everyone that's pro-choice is pro-abortion. The key word is choice. We are free to use our bodies to stab people. We are also free to use our fingers to pull triggers. It's the choices we make, right or wrong. There's too much gray area to have everything in life so cut and dry. No two situations are alike, no two people are the same. That's individuality. Like I said, my belief is my choice, and no one can force other beliefs on me. You can speak your belief as often as you like, but it's up to each individual on if they choose to agree or disagree. Choice is the freedom. By the way, I really do appreciate your opinion on this. I think it's important to engage in honest dialogue without hostility. Thank you!

Travis Rogers: I, too, very much appreciate the civil dialogue. It's nice to be able to be frank while not being rude or condescending. As for beliefs, again, it's not about beliefs. It's about absolutes. Killing the innocent is absolutely wrong. I'm sure you also believe it's wrong for a mother to down her two-year-old because she was struggling to make ends meet and thought it would be cheaper not having to buy diapers or food. If a court of law went to convict this mother, would you say you believe her to be wrong but that it's not the court's place to push their beliefs onto her when she should be free to choose whether her son lives or dies? Of course, we both already know the answer to that rhetorical question. Why, then, is the same level of consistency and value for human life not applied to the weakest and most helpless of us?

146

Jasmine: Aha...see. My point exactly. You believe it's about absolutes and I believe it's about choice and beliefs! Ergo, we agree to disagree! I have been on both sides of the table. I had a full term and put her up for adoption (because I don't believe in abortion) and my ex-husband chose to save my life by following doctor's orders with the other situation. It's definitely a touchy subject for sure. Whichever side of the spectrum you choose, I like to believe or think that all forms of life are precious. Be it human or animal.

Travis Rogers: But what of my other point? Would you hold a consistent standard in regard to the hypothetical mother who killed her two-year-old and was about to be declared guilty? What of her free choice? In cases of absolute medical necessity (which are rare and a very small percentage), I can understand it. Ectopic pregnancies are one example. Hopefully, medicine will one day advance to the point where such babies can be saved. For now, we're not quite there. However, for cases of abortion-on-demand, it amounts to the equivalent of killing a toddler or enslaving a portion of the human race. In both cases, someone declared their free choices to be of higher value than the actual life of another and are fighting to be able to dehumanize others in the name of choice.

Jasmine: Can't fix stupid. Just because you can choose to kill something or someone, doesn't make it right. It's like guns. You can do all the licensing and background stuff and follow laws to the T, but there's always going to be that one time where someone snaps or loses control. I don't have the answers for everyone or everything, I can only speak from my own experience and feelings/ beliefs, you know?

Travis Rogers: That's my point exactly! However, while the mother is free to choose to kill her two-year-old, it's not without consequences. I'm simply saying these same consequences need to apply across the board to all humans. This is why we have laws in general and don't live in a state of apathetic anarchy. Constraints are placed on illicit behavior all the time and that's a good thing. Yet society is currently telling us one should be free to kill her child and that anybody who might stand up for innocent human beings is a bully and oppressor.

Jasmine: I think the concept applies to everyone across the board, but for me, the enforcement does not because of each situation being different, you know? A malicious taking of a life is one thing. An incestuous termination in a minor through no fault of her own is another story. That's all. But yes, Hands down, killing is wrong, but in certain situations, self-defense, medical stuff..etc... the consequences should not be the same. I don't believe the people standing up are bullies. Unless they start bullying. Definitely fight for what you believe, but no one should ever hurt or oppress another just because of how they feel. It's kind of a cycle or double edge sword in way isn't it. When both sides push, some people in the middle are the ones hurt or crushed.

Travis Rogers: If it means someone gets their feelings hurt because they're told they wouldn't have the legal right to kill their children, so be it. We should always speak firmly yet softly. The truth has a way of knowing who to encourage and who to sting. I hope our society one day treats little children like they actually matter and actually have the right to life, instead of being discarded and killed at the whims of another. Any other worldview is nothing short of wicked. Sadly, abortion-on-demand doesn't stop a woman from being a mother. It just makes her the mother of a child who died at her own hands in the name of freedom of choice. It's an ugly truth that many would rather ignore while focusing on choice rather than the act they're committing. Regarding your comments on incest, I often hear this one lumped in with rape (i.e. "in cases of rape and incest"). However, a person being created as the result of rape or incest doesn't disqualify the person from personhood. They still have value and are still innocent regardless of how they came to be. Thus, taking the life of another solely because of who their father may be is still a malicious act that says a person is no longer worthy of life and deserves to be killed.

It doesn't minimize any trauma that a victim may endure and turning the victim into the assailant isn't a solution. It only compounds an existing problem.

Travis Rogers: (*sharing a photo of an article where two people are being charged with second degree murder in the death of a baby*) Here's a great example that popped into my feed just now. Should these two be charged or should they be free to choose? That's the consistency I'm referring to. Most agree these two should be charged. Yet, those same people think they should be free to kill the child if only it's a bit younger and still living in a womb. In both cases, the same child exists as a full-fledged human, just at different stages of physical development in the human lifecycle. Just as these two should be charged for choosing to freely kill another human, so should a mother who freely kills her child through abortion-on-demand. Both are guilty of the same act, yet only one child is currently protected by law.

Jasmine: Correct. But on the flip side, from the parents of the child/victim, a minor in some cases, it's a sensitive issue in whether to make them go through the process of giving birth. I can sympathize with parents not wanting their child to go through that. I don't think that they should necessarily be perceived as an assailant because, due to age, comprehension of the entire situation could be an issue. What if the victim is mentally challenged? I get what you're saying but there's still so much gray area in so many situations that again it should not be an either-or consequence. Very valid points though! Definitely. It's just tough all the way around. For all parties involved.

Travis Rogers: I grant that it is a sensitive issue, but I cannot grant that killing another human being is an acceptable outcome one should be free to choose. The fact that it is so widely accepted as a viable option is only evidence of how depraved our society has really become. No amount of external circumstance can justify murder. There are definitely many who are ignorant of what is taking place in abortion. This is because society has deceived them. However, imagine someone being deceived into thinking rape was just a game. He goes out and rapes multiple women because he thinks he has the right to do so as a game. Should he be free to rape or should he be charged with a crime? What if he doesn't believe it to be a violent crime because he feels he has the right to stick his stuff wherever he wants while playing games with the women? I think most would agree ignorance is no excuse. Most would push to have him charged for his actions regardless. What if these two (in the above photo) claim they don't think it's wrong to do what they did. Is everything forgiven since they didn't believe it was wrong? Murder is murder and abortion-on-demand is nothing less than the termination of one's life against his/her will. So long as that perspective is maintained, one can work on how to properly help someone. However, if that perspective is lost, all we're doing is turning victims into assailants (even if unwittingly, the human is still killed by their hand). Best case scenario, it promotes manslaughter in the name of healing and difficult circumstances.

Jasmine: As right as you are about the feelings being hurt, the system can't make one ring to rule them all. Every situation is not the same. Thanks again for the great conversation. Now if we can just keep other countries from eating dogs, stealing them from backyards for bait in dog fights, stealing children to sell overseas...etc.. then that too would be great. Kind regards to you and I hope you have a great rest of the day

Travis Rogers: Thanks for the great conversation. I do hope you will one day agree that killing people should be outlawed across the board. It has certainly been a pleasure dialoguing with you though. As a parting note, to put it concisely, I firmly stand by the statement that it is not okay to kill an innocent human being in cold blood when:

1) circumstances get tough

2) finances get tight

3) a traumatic event has occurred

4) the person has a physical handicap

5) the person has a mental handicap

6) the person is unloved

7) the person is unwanted

8) the person's father is a criminal

9) someone just feels like it

---

[i] WLTX, Associated Press, "Bill banning most abortions in South Carolina passes key vote," WLTX News19, February 17, 2021, https://www.wltx.com/article/news/local/bill-banning-most-abortions-in-south-carolina-passes-wednesday/101-ade04485-54f9-4875-b239-81a16919e6a9

<u>**Example #12**</u>

OPENING STATEMENT:

Nate: Imagine passing a bill telling a woman what she can or cannot do with her own body.

CONTEXT:

Response to a news article referring to a legislative bill proposing a "heartbeat bill" for the state.

DISCUSSIONS:

Travis Rogers: It's not. It's a bill telling women they can't kill another human being.

Nate: Again, not your choice or decision. Make sure you go into the hospitals and tell every woman that and see how it mulls over.

Travis Rogers: The personal opinions of other people have no bearing on the fact that abortion is the killing of the most innocent class of human being to ever exist. The fact that it's even considered a decision shows how depraved and wicked people really are. You do realize murdering someone under 18 years of age is still called murder, right? Just because you're under 18, it doesn't negate your right to life.

Nate: I can't tell you what you can or cannot do with your body. I respect a woman's decision. Period.

Travis Rogers: You just said you respect a woman's right to kill her child. Think about that one.

Nate: I respect her choice to make the life altering decision on her own. Think about that one.

Travis Rogers: And a life ending decision for an innocent person. Life ending always weighs heavier than life altering.

Nate: Maybe so, but not your decision to make.

Travis Rogers: It should be nobody's decision to make. Do you honestly believe someone should have the legal right to kill an innocent human being? Just for one second, stop looking at it through a lens of perceived women's rights and begin looking at it through a lens of actual human rights. Nobody deserves to die just because someone else feels they should have the right to kill them.

Nate: I can see it from both sides. Again, regardless of what I feel about the whole thing doesn't matter. You can try and spin it any way you want. But once someone advocates for the fetus, that means they are actually giving up the mother's right. Think about that for a second, everyone out here advocating for the fetus (which is absolutely fine), but the hypocrisy about that is that now no one cares about the women's right to her own body. That's my argument. Whether it's right or wrong, if you want human rights then you understand that the mother, a human, has rights.

Travis Rogers: I've not once advocated for the oppression of the mother or a reduction in rights to her body. I'm merely advocating for someone who is being told it's okay for them to die. If I were to use my bodily autonomy to kill you because you were sitting in a chair that I wanted to sit in, you'd be thankful laws existed prohibiting such activity. You would never say my right to do what I want with my body is more important than your basic right to life. If you want to bring up hypocrisy, that's where it's really at. I don't say that as a jab. I just mean to point out the illogical nature of it all. Yes, a mother's body is affected during pregnancy. However, a desire to be free of circumstances that negatively affect us is not enough justification to kill an innocent human being. Again, that's not oppression. That's called defending human life against the ultimate form of oppression.

Nate: then we can agree to disagree and that's fine. I respect your point of view. I do. We both just know that no matter what we say, won't affect her decision at all. That's all I'm saying.

Travis Rogers: Considering your position necessitates mothers being legally allowed to kill their children, I can't say I respect it. That said, I do respect you as a person and appreciate the civil dialogue. As for the statement that nothing we say will have any effect, I disagree. Countless lives have been saved through sidewalk ministries and Crisis Pregnancy Centers. If the use changes to protect the preborn as the humans they are, it would save countless more. However, it all starts with people being willing to speak up for the innocent and be a voice for the voiceless. I can't do it alone and I'm thankful for those who are willing to stand up with me in the fight for stopping the oppression of our most innocent class of fellow humans.

Nate: I guess my stance being her decision is also based on, if she's going to do it, I'd rather her have a safe place. At least the mother has a shot of living that way. I do appreciate the dialogue; many can't do that anymore. It's important to stick up for what you believe for sure.

Travis Rogers: I've heard the "safe place" argument before as well. However, I can't think of anyone who would promote murderers having a safe place to commit the act so that they won't have to hide from police and possibly be shot for it in an altercation. Providing a safe place for abortion is nothing more than promoting a safe place for children to be killed. Ironically, for being called a safe place, it has nearly a 100% mortality rate for the child.

Example #13

OPENING STATEMENT:

Ron: Which is why all pro-lifers support universal health care, abolishing the death penalty, strict gun laws, and police reform.

CONTEXT:

A person's response to another being thankful for pro-life educators who teach morality and continue the good fight against the ending of innocent lives through abortion.

DISCUSSIONS:

Travis Rogers: Congrats on squeezing in a many nonsequiturs and category errors as you did. Most people would've stopped at two but you decided to go above and beyond.

Ron: I come from "the rule of threes" but when it comes to preserving lives in a proactive way (you know, actually being pro-life), the more the merrier! Which reminds me: more aid for refugees. There's a book I read that talks a lot about that. Tip of my tongue. Starts with a B...

Travis Rogers: It helps to not conflate quality of life with actual life. While there are many organizations that exist to help others (many were actually founded by Christians), this is a matter of dehumanizing people and the legal ability to kill them.

Ron: Just say you care more about fetuses more than poor people because it fits your narrative. Nobody's forcing you to give a s***, but denying preventative aid because it's "socialist" or it's what you've been told to be against is hypocritical at best.

Travis Rogers: That's just a nonsequitur. Because I don't support the vast number of socialized systems in our government doesn't necessitate apathy toward the poor. However, openly supporting the murder of the preborn does necessitate apathy toward dehumanization and murder.

Ron: More people, like actual living real people, die because of people like you, than "unborn children." You actively contribute to more deaths due to your bias and apathy than a facade of apathy towards bootstraps bulls***. Be ashamed.

Travis Rogers: And, yet you provide no data or substantiation for your hollow rhetoric. Meanwhile, I have 60,000,000 dead statistics to back my claims. #followthescience

Appendix C
Pregnancy Resources

The following are resources meant to help aid pregnant women in need. Assistance can range from ultrasounds to medical care to adoptive services (and anything in between). As of printing, these resources are up to date. If you are pregnant, and are contemplating an abortion, I passionately urge you to reach out to a resource located near you to discuss associated risks as well as any possible alternatives. For your convenience, resources are broken down by state. I will attempt to include as many as I can, though it would prove too great an endeavor to list them all. To the best of my ability, I tried to add resources that will not suggest abortion as an alternative. I hope my research and discernment was successful. Just remember, you are not alone. There are many organizations out there just waiting for you to reach out. Don't see one in your area? Call any of them! I am positive they will be willing to help point you in the right direction. Let this be one of your many demonstrable acts of love toward your child.

Alabama

Hanceville
First Source for Women
(256) 352-5683
http://www.firstsourceforwomen.org/

Alaska

Wasilla
HeartReach Pregnancy Center
(907) 373-3456
https://www.heartreachalaska.com/

Arizona

Apache Junction
Hope Women's Center
(480) 983-4673
https://hopewomenscenter.org/

Flagstaff
Hope Women's Center
(928) 774-8302
https://hopewomenscenter.org/

Arkansas

Fayetteville
Loving Choices
(479) 631-6677
https://www.lovingchoices.org/

Little Rock
Arkansas Pregnancy Resource Center
(501) 227-7944
https://www.pregnancylittlerock.com/

California

Chula Vista
Silent Voices
(619) 422-0757
https://www.silentvoices.org/

Eureka
Pregnancy Care Center of the North Coast
(707) 444-0423
http://www.pcceureka.org/home.aspx

Huntington Beach
Horizon Pregnancy Clinic
(714) 897-7500
https://www.horizonpc.org/

Merced
Alpha Pregnancy Help Center
(209) 383-4700

https://alphaphc.com/

Sacramento
Alternatives Pregnancy Center
(916) 880-4040
http://alternativespc.org/

San Marcos
Birth Choice
(760) 744-1313
https://birthchoice.net/

Colorado

Pueblo
ACPC Women's Clinic
(719) 544-9312
https://www.acpcwc.org/

Connecticut

Middletown
ABC Women's Center
(860) 344-9292
https://abcwomenscenter.org/

Delaware

Georgetown
Sussex Pregnancy Care Center
(302) 856-4344
http://sussexpregnancy.com/

Florida

Clearwater
The Kimberly Home

(727) 443-0471

https://www.kimberlyhome.org/

Palm City

God's Resources, Inc.

(407) 592-7824

https://godsresourcesinc.org/

Saint Petersburg

The Next STEPP Center

(727) 896-9119

https://nextstepp.org/

Sanford

The Pregnancy Centers

(407) 323-3384

https://thepregnancycenters.com/

Georgia

Fayetteville

Fayette Pregnancy Resource Center

(770) 719-2288

https://fayetteprc.com/

Rincon

Pregnancy Care Center of Rincon

(912) 826-1133

https://pregnancycarecenterofrincon.com/

Hawaii

Kailua Kona

The Pregnancy Center

(808) 326-1766

http://www.tpckona.com/

Waipahu
A Place for Women in Waipio Center
(808) 678-3991
https://www.oahupregnancycenter.com/

Idaho

Bonners Ferry
A Blessed Beginning
(208) 267-1491
https://adoptanewbeginning.org/pregnant/pregnancy-services/

Illinois

Charleston
Choices Pregnancy and Health
(217) 345-5000
https://choices4pregnancy.com/

Rockford
The Pregnancy Care Center of Rockford
(815) 997-1200
https://thepregnancycarecenter.org/

Indiana

Lafayette
Matrix LifeCare
(765) 742-1533
https://www.matrixcares.org/

Iowa

Ames
Informed Choices Medical Clinic
(515) 864-8012
https://www.informedchoicesclinic.com/

Bettendorf
Women's Choice Center
(563) 332-0475
https://womenschoicecenter.org/

Davenport
Pregnancy Resources
(563) 386-3737
https://qcpregnancy.org/

Kansas

Ottawa
Life Care Center
(785) 242-4500
https://lifecarecenter.org/

Kentucky

Madisonville
Door of Hope
(270) 821-9825
http://www.doorofhope.com/

Paducah
Hope Unlimited Family Care Center
(270) 442-1166
https://hopeunlimitedfcc.org/

Louisiana

Amite
Women's Life Ministries
(985) 747-0602
http://www.womenslifeministries.org/

Maine

Augusta
Open Arms Pregnancy Center
(207) 620-1600
http://www.openarmspc.org/

Mechanic Falls
Hope House
(207) 345-3027
http://www.hopehousemaine.com/

Maryland

Silver Spring
Centro Tepeyac Women's Center
(301) 946-1022
https://centrotepeyac.org/en/

Massachusetts

Attleboro
Abundant Hope Pregnancy Resource Center
(508) 455-0425
https://ahprc.org/

Michigan

Bad Axe
Positive Alternatives
(989) 269-6760
https://mypositivealternative.com/

Battle Creek
Alternatives
(269) 288-2890
https://www.alternativescc.org/

Kalamazoo

Alternatives
(269) 345-1740
https://www.alternativescc.org/

Minnesota

Cannon Falls
Life Choice Pregnancy Resource Center
(507) 263-8000
http://lifechoicecf.org/

Park Rapids
Pregnancy Resource Center
(218) 732-5212
https://www.prcparkrapids.org/

Mississippi

Picayune
Sav-A-Life Pregnancy Support Services
(601) 799-2668
http://savalifems.org/

Missouri

Clinton
Door of Hope Pregnancy Center
(660) 890-7011
https://gvdoorofhope.org/

Grain Valley
If Not For Grace Ministries
(816) 847-2911
https://www.infg.org/

Macon
Ray of Hope Pregnancy Care

(660) 395-8099

https://www.rayofhopepregnancycenter.com/

Montana

Missoula

Life Net of Missoula

(406) 549-0406

https://www.carenetmissoula.org/

Nebraska

Omaha

Beginnings Pregnancy Resource Center

(402) 336-4343

https://beginningspregnancycenter.com/

Nevada

Carson City

Life Choices Community Pregnancy Clinic

(775) 885-1700

https://lifechoicescarson.com/

New Hampshire

Concord

CareNet Pregnancy Center

(603) 224-7477

http://www.carenetconcord.com/

Nashua

Real Options

(603) 883-1122

https://realoptionsnh.org/

New Jersey

Englewood
Gift of Hope
(201) 567-3500
http://ourgiftofhope.org

Old Bridge
Bridge Women's Center
(732) 588-0999
https://www.bridgewomenscenter.com/

New Mexico

Albuquerque
Pregnant Help Online
(505) 880-0882
http://www.pregnanthelponline.com/

New York

Troy
Alight Care Center
(518) 270-5540
https://alight.org/

North Carolina

Denver
Heartbeats
(704) 489-0708
https://heartbeatspcc.org/

Morehead City
Coastal Pregnancy Care Center
(252) 247-2273
https://cpccenter.org/

Rocky Mount

Your Choice Resource Center
(252) 446-2273
https://www.yourchoicenc.org/

Yadkinville
Compassion Care
(336) 679-7101
https://c3yadkin.com/

North Dakota

Minot
Dakota Hope Clinic
(701) 852-4673
https://dakotahope.org/

Ohio

Chillicothe
Elizabeth's Hope Pregnancy Resource Center
(740) 772-4372
http://www.thereishopetoday.org/index.html

Oklahoma

Bartlesville
The Cottage of Bartlesville
(918) 214-8854
https://www.cottageforlife.com/

Yukon
Gateway Express Testing
(405) 354-4283
https://myget.clinic/

Oregon

Lebanon
Pregnancy Alternatives Center
(541) 258-3530
pregnancyalternatives.org/

Medford
The Pregnancy Center
(541) 772-1921
https://thepregnancycenter.us/

Pennsylvania

Philadelphia
AlphaCare
(215) 545-4673
https://alphacarephilly.org/

Rhode Island

Providence
CareNet Pregnancy Center of Rhode Island
(401) 941-4357
https://www.carenetri.com/

South Carolina

Columbia
Daybreak Ministries
(803) 771-6634
https://www.daybreakcola.org/

South Dakota

Spearfish
Bella Pregnancy Resource Center
(605) 642-4140
https://bellapregnancy.com/

Tennessee

Jackson
Birth Choice
(731) 664-8443
https://www.birthchoice.biz/

Maryville
Pregnancy Resource Center
(865) 977-8378
https://prcbctn.com/

Texas

Beaumont
Hope Women's Resource Clinic
(409) 898-4005
https://www.hope-clinic.com/

Decatur
Wise Choices Pregnancy Resource Center
(940) 627-6924
http://mywisechoices.com/

El Paso
Southwest Coalition for Life
(833) 388-5433
(915) 249-1344
https://pfsep.org/

Kerrville
First Choice Reproductive Health
(830) 315-4541
https://firstchoicerh.com/

San Antonio
A Woman's Haven

(210) 224-2902

https://awomanshaven.com/

Utah

Moab

Arches News Hope Pregnancy Center

(435) 259-5433

http://archesnewhope.org/

St. George

Hope Pregnancy Care Center

(435) 652-8343

https://hopepregnancyutah.org/

Vermont

Barre

CareNet Pregnancy Center

(802) 479-9215

https://carenetcv.org/

Virginia

Charlottesville

Thrive Women's Healthcare

(434) 979-8888

https://thrivecentralva.org/

Chesapeake

Crisis Pregnancy Center of Tidewater

(757) 410-9703

https://cpcfriends.org/

Culpeper

Thrive Women's Healthcare

(540) 727-0400

https://thrivecentralva.org/

Washington

Tacoma
CareNet Pregnancy & Family Resources of Puget Sound
(206) 926-7860
https://carenetps.org/

West Virginia

Bluefield
Abel Crisis Pregnancy Center
(304) 325-8694
https://www.abelcenter.org/

Wisconsin

Antigo
Hope Life Center
(715) 843-4673
https://www.hopewi.org/

Milwaukee
Milwaukee Birthright
(414) 672-5433
http://milwaukeebirthright.com/

Wyoming

Cheyenne
Life Choice Pregnancy Care Center
(307) 632-6323
https://www.lifechoicepcc.org/

Additional Resources

Save the Storks

Mobile pregnancy centers offering ultrasounds and counseling
https://savethestorks.com/

Special Supplemental Nutrition Program for Women, Infants, and Children (WIC)

Provides federal grants to states for supplemental foods, health care referrals, and nutrition education for low-income pregnant, breastfeeding, and non-breastfeeding postpartum women.
https://www.fns.usda.gov/wic

ABOUT THE AUTHOR

Travis W. Rogers is a diligent student of the Word and faithfully served in the U.S. Navy for 20 years (2000 - 2020), retiring as a Chief Petty Officer. From 2008-2017, he acted as Protestant Lay Leader onboard multiple Navy warships and led others in their spiritual walk both in the absence of and alongside a Chaplain. It has been his deepest desire to see others come to the knowledge of truth and experience a deeper walk with God. He is the author of multiple books and frequently writes articles for The Particular Baptist blog (theparticularbaptist.net). Travis and his wife, Tiffany, are blessed to have a son and two daughters, and are members of Covenant Reformed Baptist Church in Warrenton, VA.

Made in the USA
Monee, IL
12 August 2021